Hope for the Violently Aggressive Child

New Diagnoses and Treatments that Work

❧ ❦

Dr. Ralph Ankenman

All marketing and publishing rights guaranteed to and reserved by:

FUTURE HORIZONS INC.

721 W. Abram Street

Arlington, TX 76013

800•489•0727

817•277•0727

817•277•2270 (fax)

E-mail: *info@fhautism.com*

www.fhautism.com

Illustrations prepared by Malinda Lowder

ISBN: 978-1-935274-87-2

Printed in the United States of America

All statements in this book are solely those of the author. No pharmaceutical company, corporation, organization, or institution had involvement, input, interest or sponsorship in the substance of this book. To protect privacy, patient names are changed, except in cases of explicit permission.

Contents

❧❧

Foreword by Temple Grandin, PhD i

Introduction iii

A Violently Aggressive Child vii

Survey of Aggressive Behavior Symptoms (Sometimes Identified with Bipolar Disorder in Children) xi

PART I: THE EPIDEMIC OVERDIAGNOSIS OF BIPOLAR DISORDER IN CHILDREN 17

    Chapter 1: The Increasing Diagnosis of Childhood Bipolar Disorder in America 19

    Chapter 2: Bipolar Disorder: What It Is, and What It Isn't 27

PART II: INSTINCTS AND VIOLENT AGGRESSION 33

    Chapter 3: Behavior Problems in Children Caused by Adrenaline System Over-Reactivity 35

    Chapter 4: Instincts and Adrenaline Crisis 43

    Chapter 5: Two Systems of Adrenaline Reactivity 51

    Chapter 6: Two Adrenaline Crisis States 63

PART III: CASE STUDIES AND CLINICAL EXPERIENCES 67

    Chapter 7: Adrenaline and Behavioral Science: Case Studies and Medical Literature 69

    Chapter 8: When a Child Has Rage Reactions as Well as Another Diagnosis 107

    Chapter 9: Bipolar Disorder Revisited 113

PART IV: TALKING TO CLINICIANS 123

    Chapter 10: Collecting Information 125

    Chapter 11: Other Treatment Considerations 131

Medication Addendum 137

Postscript by Dr. Edward Cutler 147

Excerpted Transcript Telephone Conversation Between Kayla and Dr. Ankenman on June 29, 2011 155

Works Cited 163

"I just want my child back."

"There is a group of children with severe irritability or affective aggression or rages whose explosive behavior is significantly impairing, that we have been chasing with different diagnoses over the years, that populate child psychiatry clinics, and that we haven't had a great deal of success in treating."

Acknowledgements

I wish to thank the many friends and relatives who offered help and advice as I prepared this material. Special thanks to my editor Carol Hommel and to her husband David for website and business assistance. Dr. Edward Cutler's association over the last three years helped confirm the validity of this new treatment regime. I also thank the parents and caregivers of patients through the years who patiently provided the information that helped me define and clarify these clinical understandings. My wife, Dr. E. Lucille Ankenman, has supported me and my medical career in a multitude of ways that are not adequately captured in words.

For all the affected children like Bob and Abby, and for their parents

Foreword by
Temple Grandin, PhD

❧ ❦

THERE is a tendency for some doctors to overmedicate children with autism, attention-deficit/hyperactivity disorder, and many other disorders. This most likely occurs when parents and teachers are at their wits' end on how to deal with a child who has severe behavioral problems. When medications are used in a careful, conservative manner, they can be really helpful. In my early 30s, when anxiety and panic attacks were tearing me apart, a low dose of antidepressants saved me. Antidepressants were a miracle for me. When antidepressants are used for anxiety, it is important to use a low dose. If the dose of Prozac, Zoloft, or Lexapro is too high, the child may have agitation and insomnia. Too often, doctors raise the dose of an antidepressant, when they should be lowering it.

Today, way too many children are being given powerful atypical antipsychotic drugs, when they do not need them. These drugs have more severe side effects than antidepressants do. Drugs with fewer side effects should be tried first.

For some children with violent or aggressive behavior, blood pressure medicines that are much safer to use may help stop severe aggression. This is not going to work for every child, but there are some individuals who can benefit from the information in Dr Ralph Ankenman's book.

Hope for the Violently Aggressive Child

He discusses the use of blood pressure medicines, such as alpha blockers and beta blockers, for treatment of severe aggression. All parents and professors who have to work with children and/or adults who have severe aggression problems should read this book. Many of the drugs that Dr Ankenman discusses are cheap generics that may be really helpful. Little research has been done with cheap generic blood pressure medications because there is no profit incentive. I can remember two nonverbal boys who, years ago, were saved from being institutionalized by taking the blood pressure medicine propranodol. For some children, the information in this book may help a physician prescribe safer, more effective medications to control violent behavior. Blood pressure medications will not work for every individual. The factors that cause violent and aggressive behavior are very variable.

There are some children with aggressive behavior who will make the most improvement when the careful use of medication is combined with placing boundaries on behavior. When I had a tantrum, my mother consistently enforced the rule of no television for one night. This prevented many outbursts. The consequences have to be very consistent because a child will often keep testing the boundaries. For some children, this book may provide effective strategies.

— *Temple Grandin, PhD*

Author of The Way I See It
and The Autistic Brain

Introduction

❧❧

THE main purpose of this book is to offer effective treatment options for an urgent problem in America—children with episodes of violent aggression.

The diagnosis of bipolar disorder in children has soared. That trend has been controversial and has presented many unanswered questions, particularly when a child's problems primarily involve "violent meltdowns" rather than mania or depression. American children diagnosed with bipolar disorder in recent years should be re-evaluated for an altogether different condition that I call "adrenaline system over-reactivity." This condition is related to immaturity rather than a mental disorder, and it can be treated with medications that have fewer side effects and less intrusion on a child's mental function than the medicines prescribed for bipolar disorder.

It is fundamental to understand the relationship between aggressive behavior and immature adrenaline reactivity in order to treat the behavior effectively. Thus far, treatment strategies—including medical, behavioral, and dietary approaches—do not directly address the adrenaline-based reactivity that causes the behavior to escalate out of control.

A broader purpose of this book is to increase understanding about how adrenaline system activity impacts behavior in general. I would like to focus attention and encourage research on a question that modern medicine has not been asking: "What is the role of adrenaline stress in behavioral medicine?" This is an important direction for the future of behavioral science, particularly in children, whose physical and mental maturation is vulnerable and incomplete.

Human aggression is directly related to activation of the body's adrenaline systems. Adrenaline activity is a natural physical response that can produce threatening, attacking, agitated, or violently aggressive behavior in times of crisis or extreme danger.

Certain children have immature over-arousal of the adrenaline systems. They experience surges of adrenaline even when they are not in life-threatening situations. When this happens, their bodies have intense physical changes like a pounding heart, and intense mental changes like a loss of rational control. These changes play a major role in the intensity and momentum of their episodes. Adrenaline over-arousal can cause behavior so extreme that it can be mistaken for symptoms of a mental disorder, yet the role of the adrenaline systems is not considered when parents seek professional help.

I authored this book primarily as a description of my own 30+ years of clinical experience treating patients with aggressive and violent behavior. When I use the term "we," I am referencing my collaboration with pediatrician Dr. Edward Cutler. In recent years, we have shared information, especially about the use of adrenaline-acting medicines for treatment of aggression. We have seen many patients mature to the point that they no longer needed medication.

To date, there are no studies published that would make this treatment approach more widely available. It is my hope that this book will bring relief to those with behavior problems caused by adrenaline over-arousal and provide new options for parents and physicians attempting to care for

INTRODUCTION

children with intractable episodes of violent aggression. If some clinicians learn the effectiveness of adrenaline-acting medicines, researchers may conduct the studies necessary for their use to become more accepted.

Treatment of childhood aggression in America can be revolutionized if adrenaline system over-arousal becomes a standard consideration. Many children could have more effective, less expensive, and possibly curative treatment without psychiatric diagnoses and without psychiatric medications.

— *Ralph Ankenman, M.D.*

A Violently Aggressive Child

❧ ❧

TYLER was seven years old when I met him. His uncontrollable episodes of aggressive behavior had started when he was four. He had been given several different diagnoses and medicine combinations. He had been tried on high doses of different psychiatric drugs. His grandmother told me that nothing worked for any length of time. She described episodes this way:

> ... he had violent, blind rages to the point he seemed possessed. They would last until he wore himself out and just fell over asleep. He was not able to stay in school for more than two or three hours at a time and he was so violent that we couldn't handle him even at home. We had to hospitalize him because it got so bad. In the past two and a half years he has been hospitalized nine times. He has been in four different facilities. He would come home for short periods—some- times days—and then it would start all over again and he would have to be readmitted.

Tyler was in the hospital when his grandmother heard of my treatment approach through a local newspaper article. Four months passed before he returned home. A week later, his grandmother brought him to see me because his aggressive episodes were already starting to re-appear.

I placed Tyler on two medications that stabilize adrenaline system activity. The severity and frequency of his rage reactions decreased quickly.

Hope for the Violently Aggressive Child

Within a month, he returned to school for full days. He has not required re-admission to the hospital since starting the medications. His grandmother says:

It has not been an easy road, but this is the longest Tyler has stayed out of the hospital for the past two and a half years. Dr. Ankenman hopes that with maturity, he will be able to get off all or most of the medicines. I know he has given Tyler a chance at life because for the past few months, Tyler has been able to be in society.

People use different terms to describe aggressive episodes in children, including "meltdowns," "tantrums," "fits," "aggression" and "rages." That is why all of those terms appear somewhere in this book.

I use the phrase "violently aggressive" because I am referring to situations beyond the occasional temper tantrum or angry outburst that all children will have in the course of growing up. I am referring to behavior that is so frequent, intense, or out-of-control that the child's function at home and school is compromised.

A significant number of children who have explosive, violent meltdowns have been misdiagnosed as having bipolar disorder, when their destructive, antisocial, "scary" behavior is caused instead by immature and excessive adrenaline system reactivity.

For a variety of reasons, certain children have surges of adrenaline that cause them to lose rational control and develop intense physical agitation or rage. They look or seem to have "temporary insanity" because they lose the ability to be socially appropriate, and they do things unusual for their personality like cursing and threatening to harm or kill people whom they love.

The following behavior survey should give you some idea whether the information and treatments discussed in this book might be relevant to your child. It will also give you something to discuss with his or her doctor or other caregivers.

Survey of Aggressive Behavior Symptoms (Sometimes Identified with Bipolar Disorder in Children)

PUT a mark beside behaviors that could describe your child during an aggressive episode. Following the survey are explanations about the different groups of behavior symptoms.

Check if "Yes"

1	☐	The child has explosions of sudden anger when frustrated.
2	☐	During episodes, the child has mostly random, unfocused hitting out at whatever is nearby (others, objects, or himself/ herself).
3	☐	During episodes, the child becomes flushed (face or body reddens).
4	☐	Afterwards, the child says that he/she tried to stop but could not.

5	☐	Afterwards, the child apologizes.
6	☐	Certain adults can calm the child quickly (either by talking to or holding the child).
7	☐	The child complains that his or her heart was beating fast or hurting during the episode.
8	☐	During episodes or when excited, the child has hand or finger tremor (fingers or hands shake slightly).
9	☐	The child has a habit of biting or picking at fingernails or skin.
10	☐	During episodes, the child is unusually strong.
11	☐	The child is very physically active as part of his or her normal personality (i.e., rarely sits still even while watching television).
12	☐	The child tends to run a high resting heart rate (90 beats per minute or above).
13	☐	During episodes, the child has "crazy" or "evil" looking eyes. Eyes may appear dilated, unfocused, or nonresponsive.

SURVEY OF AGGRESSIVE BEHAVIOR SYMPTOMS

14	☐	During episodes, the child's personality seems changed, for example, becoming hateful with swearing and threatening.
15	☐	During episodes, the child threatens to kill or harm others or claims to hate people who he or she loves.
16	☐	After episodes, the child does not apologize or seem remorseful.
17	☐	After episodes, the child denies certain behaviors that happened.
18	☐	After episodes, the child seems not to remember the whole event.
19	☐	During episodes, the child becomes more violent if there is any attempt to hold or restrain him or her.
20	☐	The child's aggression seems focused and deliberate toward particular people or targets.
21	☐	The child has anger episodes that move from being anxious and upset to getting wild-eyed and "going crazy."
22	☐	The child will suddenly have an extreme increase in energy and activity that lasts for several days or weeks in a row.

23	☐	During times of extreme energy and activity, the child will sleep fewer hours without acting tired (several days or weeks in a row).
24	☐	The child's changes in mood happen for no apparent reason, not in response to events or people around him or her.
25	☐	The child has times of intense and unrealistic feelings that everyone is against him or her.
26	☐	The child's mood changes suddenly from several days of extreme activity to several days in a row of completely normal personality.
27	☐	During periods of extreme activity or a mood change, the child has wild and unrealistic ideas about his or her own abilities.

Items 1–12 = symptoms of adrenaline over-reactivity (beta type)
Items 13–21 = symptoms of adrenaline over-reactivity (alpha type)
Items 22–27 = bipolar disorder symptoms

The first twelve items describe symptoms of excessive adrenaline arousal (beta type), and behaviors 13–21 describe symptoms of excessive adrenaline arousal (alpha type). These states are not necessarily signs of mental illness— they are signs of immaturity in the child's adrenaline reactivity. Children have natural, primitive "emergency" adrenaline reflexes that they learn to control as they grow up. In some children these reflexes remain immature, and they are not able to prevent the adrenaline surge from escalating into a state of violent aggression. Part II of the book explains what happens in a child's body when excessive adrenaline is released, and how those changes can lead to episodes of violent aggression. Part II also explains how to identify the different behavioral and physical symptoms of "beta" versus "alpha" adrenergic over-arousal.

The last six behaviors on the survey specifically relate to classic bipolar disorder. If none of the last six behaviors are relevant to a child's situation, the diagnosis of bipolar disorder is not highly likely. However, there is ongoing research and debate about bipolar symptoms in children. A brief overview of bipolar disease and the controversies surrounding its diagnosis in children is discussed in Part I.

PART I

THE EPIDEMIC OVERDIAGNOSIS OF BIPOLAR DISORDER IN CHILDREN

CHAPTER 1

The Increasing Diagnosis of Childhood Bipolar Disorder in America

৵৽

THE RISE OF THE DIAGNOSIS IN AMERICA BUT NOT ELSEWHERE

WHEN I started writing this book in the summer of 2010, a Google search of the three words "bipolar," "children," and "over diagnosis" produced over 128,000 results. A search for the phrase "bipolar epidemic" brought 1,800 hits, and by the time I was ready to send the book to print, that number nearly doubled.

To those working in psychiatry or education, or to those who have a child diagnosed with bipolar disorder, it is not news to announce there is controversy surrounding the increase in the number of children in America diagnosed with bipolar disorder. Debate became more intense with the publication of the September 2007 issue of *The Archives of General Psychiatry*, which included a study reporting the 40-fold increase in the diagnosis of bipolar disorder in children between 1994 and 2003.[1] The controversy remains alive as experts debate how the issue should be

---

1. Moreno C., Laje G, Blanco C., Jiang H., Schmidt A., Olfson M. "National trends in the outpatient diagnosis and treatment of bipolar disorder in youth." *Arch Gen Psychiatry*. 2007; 64(9):1032-1039.

addressed in the upcoming fifth edition of the American Psychiatric Association's "Diagnostic and Statistical Manual of Mental Disorders" (DSM-V), due for release in May 2013.

Voices from inside and outside the medical community raise a variety of concerns about the "bipolar epidemic:"

1. Are children being misdiagnosed?
2. Was bipolar disease in children previously under-diagnosed?
3. Is the phenomenon explained by "early onset" bipolar disorder?
4. Why are children with primary symptoms of anger and aggression being diagnosed with bipolar?
5. Should the psychiatric profession create a new, separate diagnosis in the DSM-V for children whose symptoms fall outside standard bipolar criteria?

Credible authorities have differing views. The patients are children whose physical and mental systems are still developing. Clinicians generally are hesitant to label a child with a mental disorder that would call for lifelong treatment with psychiatric medicines. Many clinicians admit openly that in the absence of better treatment alternatives, "bipolar disorder" is a convenient option for treating children whose severely aggressive behavior is socially intolerable. Doctors are not likely to say to a parent, "I understand that your child is violently attacking you and his teachers several times a week, but that doesn't qualify as a mental disorder, so go on home and live with that."

---

2. Post R.M., Luckenbaugh D.A., Leverich G.S., Altshuler L.L., Frye M.A., Suppes T., Keck P.E., McElroy S.L., Nolen W.A., Kupka R., Grunze H., Walden J. "Incidence of childhood-onset bipolar illness in the USA and Europe." *Br J Psychiatry.* 2008 Feb; 192(2):150-1.

CHAPTER 1

It is worth noting that the sharp increase in children diagnosed with bipolar in the past decade or so is seen only in America. The rate of childhood bipolar disorder has not risen equivalently in other countries, even in Europe.[2] That fact appears to support the opinion of those who believe that the bipolar diagnosis is used too often in the United States.

Regardless of disagreements over diagnosis, there seems to be agreement that the number of American children with behavior that is exceptionally difficult to deal with socially and to treat medically has dramatically increased in the past twenty years. In increasing numbers, children have been brought to doctors or hospitals because of aggressive behaviors. Complaints commonly include violence, disobedience, and physical acting-out, with extreme changes in mood. During violent episodes, some children appear "crazy" or "wild-eyed." They swear, threaten, or say hateful things that are not normal for their personality. Many do not seem to remember the episodes. Other children not only remember the events, but are genuinely apologetic afterwards. Some children become even more aggressive and violent when adults try to intervene, while others calm down when held or comforted by a trusted caregiver.

Other commonly described behaviors include an excessive need for attention, moving whimsically from one thing to another, demanding to have their own way, and wantonly attacking authority figures—especially when restricted or denied what they want.

When children exhibit behavior so disruptive that they cannot function consistently at school or even in their own home, parents seek professional help. Thus, an increasing number of medical practitioners and behavioral therapists across the country have been asked to address these severe problems—much of the time after standard behavioral programming techniques have been exhausted. Here are some statements you may recognize:

- "How can my daughter be so sweet, then suddenly look so evil?"
- "Why does she attack me for no reason?"
- "Why does my son tell me how much he loves me, but screams at me when I say 'no'?"
- "I know your son isn't a bad kid, but he can't stay in class if he can't control himself!"
- "You would not believe some of the words that come out of her mouth!"
- "Why does he have a meltdown at school nearly every day?"
- "She really doesn't want to act like that—sometimes she just loses control."

The difficulties of treating children with such episodes, and the reality that "an ill-fitting diagnosis can be more helpful than no diagnosis at all" are well described in an article published in the March 2010 issue of Child & Adolescent Psychiatry and Mental Health titled "Controversies concerning the diagnosis and treatment of bipolar disorder in children."[3] This article summarizes events of a 2008 workshop funded by the National Institute of Mental Health (NIMH) with experts including "child psychiatrists, psychologists, philosophers, sociologists, anthropologists, and others." After workshop discussions, presentations, and an extensive review of the literature, the authors concluded they "were persuaded that the (bipolar) label may fit poorly many of the children who have received it over the last decade." One child psychiatrist at the workshop commented that "there is

---

3. Parens E., Johnston J. "Controversies concerning the diagnosis and treatment of bipolar disorder in children." Child Adolesc *Psychiatry Ment Health*. 2010 Mar 10; 4:9.

CHAPTER 1

a group of children with severe irritability or affective aggression or rages whose explosive behavior is significantly impairing, that we have been chasing with different diagnoses over the years, that populate child psychiatry clinics, and that we haven't had a great deal of success in treating."

I agree with the observation that there is a group of children whose dysfunctional behavior tends to be labeled and treated according to whatever is the diagnosis du jour, which in recent years has been bipolar disorder.

The most recent pediatric "epidemic" prior to this one involved attention deficit hyperactivity disorder (ADHD). The increase in this diagnosis was fueled partially by a social and institutional need for services: a medication treatment regimen for the child, an identified label for claiming and reimbursing services, a pathway for school and caregiver behavior plans, and a support network for parents. While many children were helped by identification and therapy for untreated ADHD, others were misdiagnosed or had additional problems associated with stimulant medications.

Likewise, the diagnosis of bipolar disorder in children has been misapplied for a variety of behavior problems that do not fit coherently into current diagnostic categories or treatments. The diagnosis became the newest option for difficult pediatric cases. Admittedly, it has addressed some much-needed gaps in care. Some parents whose children were not responsive to ADHD treatments wisely investigated the new diagnosis of bipolar disorder as a potential source of help. The diagnosis can look quite legitimate in a significant number of patients. The medications used to treat bipolar disorder may reduce aggressive behavior episodes somewhat, even in children who do not have true bipolar disorder.

Certain features and safeguards built into the American medical and educational systems contribute to the creation of diagnosis "epidemics."

Hope for the Violently Aggressive Child

Physicians who treat children, especially child psychiatrists, have long been under a strict code that medicine should not be prescribed without the diagnosis of a serious illness. Likewise, schools do not offer individualized plans or modification of standard behavior expectations without a medical diagnosis.

Educators, parents, hospitals, caregivers, physicians, child advocacy groups, law enforcement, and many others must invest significant time and resources when children are out of control. By the time parents bring a child to a physician because of highly disruptive behavior that has not responded well to standard behavior plans, they come with a set of expectations: a) an expectation that some kind of illness may underlie the behavior, b) an expectation that the physician will recognize the illness, c) an expectation that medication can be prescribed to abate the symptoms, and d) an expectation that plans will be authorized so that the child can function consistently at daycare or school.

At this point, it is important to note that I am not stating that children cannot or do not have bipolar disorder; some do. Research is underway looking at potential childhood onset of bipolar disease previously unrecognized. Additionally, emerging research indicates that emotional agitation, mood dysregulation, and other behavioral issues in childhood may

---

4. Post R.M., Weiss S.R. "A speculative model of affective illness cyclicity based on patterns of drug tolerance observed in amygdala-kindled seizures." *Mol Neurobiol.* 1996 Aug; 13(1):33-60.

5. Post R.M. "Kindling and sensitization as models for affective episode recurrence, cyclicity, and tolerance phenomena." *Neurosci Biobehav* Rev. 2007, 31(6):858-73. Epub 2007; Apr 24.

6. Note that in March 2011, after I had finished writing Part I, a psychiatry professor named Dr. Stuart Kaplan published the book *Your Child Does Not Have Bipolar Disorder: How Bad Science and Good Public Relations Created the Diagnosis.* That title may indicate that the medical community is becoming increasingly skeptical of the broad application of the diag- nosis of bipolar disorder in children.

trigger or otherwise make the development of mental disease in adult-hood more likely.[4&5] At the same time, the medical community is failing to recognize situations where the diagnosis has not been reached in a meaningful way.[6]

Caught up in this epidemic are a percentage of children whose symptoms primarily involve oppositional and belligerent behavior with explosive rage reactions or tantrums, without classic symptoms of mania or spontaneous extended mood swings. For such children, the bipolar diagnosis should give us serious pause, as should treatment with antipsychotic and mood-stabilizing medications. Is the diagnosis strong enough to risk long-term impact on a child's still-developing brain? Many psychiatric medicines interfere with thinking and reasoning. How might the child's personal and social identity be affected? Side effects of some of the newer antipsychotic medications can include the increased tendency for weight gain and diabetes, already a serious social and physical consideration for America's children.

MANY CHILDREN DIAGNOSED AS "BIPOLAR" MAY NOT HAVE A LONG-TERM PSYCHIATRIC ILLNESS

Many children currently being treated under the diagnosis of bipolar disorder are exhibiting symptoms of immature adrenaline system over-reactivity and not a mental disorder. Bipolar disorder is a recognized diagnosis in which children can become psychotic sometimes and behave normally at other times. Because children can look or act psychotic during their rage episodes, it is not surprising that many physicians conclude that have childhood onset bipolar disorder. Most physicians do not recognize that episodes of severe, agitated aggression in a child can be the expression of innate reflexes that every human brain has for times of extreme crisis. In children, over-reactivity of these adrenaline "crisis reflexes" can result in episodes of pathological- looking behavior, because the child's rational controls are not fully developed.

This turns the pediatric bipolar debate in a new direction, providing a reasonable explanation for a segment of the misdiagnosed bipolar population. Treating episodic aggression with medications to address excessive adrenaline reactivity is far less intrusive for children than long-term psychiatric medications. Many of these children could greatly reduce or even resolve their behavioral problems if given medications to stabilize their adrenaline system reactivity. Agitation and aggression can be the result of natural human survival instincts, and adrenaline-acting medicines can address those arousal states directly.

Adrenaline-acting medicines specifically target the excess output of the neurochemicals triggering the child's episode, and the daily dose can be adjusted so that the hormone is blocked only to the extent that the child can function more "normally." Indeed, some children can outgrow adrenaline system over-reactivity with medication treatment, time, and behavioral help.

Certain children have pure bipolar symptoms and need long-term treatment with mood stabilizers and antipsychotics, but such cases are not very common.

The next chapter explains more about bipolar disorder—what it is and what it is not. To read more about adrenaline system over-reactivity and how excessive adrenaline arousal can lead to aggressive behavior, go to Part II.

CHAPTER 2

Bipolar Disorder:
What It Is, and What It Isn't

AN HISTORICAL OVERVIEW
OF BIPOLAR DISORDER

IT is common knowledge that some people have mood swings that go beyond ordinary ups and downs. Since ancient times every human culture has had members whose behavior suddenly changed to be so far outside normal that it seemed the person had been struck by sickness or some other affliction. "Bipolar disorder" is the most current label for the mental illness involving cycles of extreme mood swings. It is one of the two major psychotic breaks found in all cultures all over the world (the other is schizophrenia).

The term "psychotic break" is generally used for the first time psychosis takes over a person's entire brain function. "Psychosis" means a state of radical impairment in thought and function, with significant changes from the person's normal personality and perception of reality.

Bipolar disorder used to be called "manic-depression." That term was coined by Emil Kraepelin, the nineteenth-century German physician who first distinguished between the two major psychiatric breaks. Dr. Kraepelin is considered by many to be the father of modern psychiatry. The pattern of symptoms that Kraepelin identified as distinct to manic-depression involved cycling of "high" moods called mania, and low "depressed" moods, with periods of normal mood interspersed between them.[7] At some point, the term "bipolar affective disorder" became preferred to "manic-depression," probably because it sounds less negative.

The American Psychiatric Association's book titled "Diagnostic and Statistical Manual of Mental Disorders" (DSM-IV) provides today's medical professionals with official criteria for diagnosing bipolar disorder. The DSM-IV discusses rapid cycling, hypomania, and all manner of complicated symptom combinations that are not very easy to read or comprehend without special training. At the risk of oversimplification, there are five characteristics that distinguish the pattern of bipolar symptoms from other mental illnesses. An individual psychiatric symptom like depression may be present in several different disorders.

DISTINGUISHING BIPOLAR DISORDER
FROM OTHER PSYCHIATRIC ILLNESSES

The following are five characteristics unique to bipolar disorder:

1. It generally begins with a sudden psychotic break
2. It involves one or more manic episodes
3. It tends to involve times of completely normal function between mood swings
4. Moods generally last for days or weeks (not hours)
5. A change in mood comes on unpredictably, not necessarily related to a specific circumstance or event.

---

7. Kraepelin, Emil. "Manic-Depressive Insanity and Paranoia" translated into English 1921. www.onread.com/book/Manic-Depressive-Insanity-And-Paranoia-82583

CHAPTER 2

All five of these symptoms may not be present together in a given patient. However, without a history of some of these distinguishing symptoms, most clinicians would not consider a diagnosis of bipolar disorder to be more likely than other possible diagnoses like Post-traumatic Stress Disorder, intermittent explosive disorder, borderline personality, or chronic depression.

1. *Bipolar disorder generally begins with a sudden psychotic break.*

A true psychotic break results in a complete change in mental status and function. For example, a person having a psychotic break may suddenly believe they have a very important social position or duty to perform. They are convinced that they are, or should be, at the center of everyone's social attention, and they are unable to realize that their thoughts are not rational.

A classic example of a bipolar break would be a man who suddenly quits his job "to write the great American novel," then goes home and writes for thirty-six hours without stopping. What he writes may not be very coherent. But while he is manic, he has no ability to judge the quality of his work. What he is doing seems perfect to him, and he fully expects others to recognize its perfection. (The other psychotic break, a schizophrenic break, often involves social isolation. Such individuals perceive themselves as uniquely involved with powerful individuals or agencies, often with the paranoid idea that some powerful force is out to get them.)

Most people having a bipolar psychotic break have what is called manic psychosis. They become hyperactive and hyper-"energized." Untreated, a psychotic break could last for weeks or months—which is exactly what used to happen before modern psychiatric medications were developed. Modern antipsychotic medications "slow down" the brain and help it more quickly regain use of its rational controls and normal relationship with the outside world.

2. Bipolar disorder involves one or more manic episodes.

Even if a patient does not have an initial psychotic break, there should be evidence of at least one episode of mania to diagnose bipolar disorder. Manic episodes are unique to bipolar disorder. They represent a period of excessive physical and mental energy during which a person loses normal social perspective and self-restraint. During a manic episode, a person may go for extended periods without sleep or food without feeling tired or weak. They may spend money foolishly, stay up all night cleaning or baking, or become excessively sexual. Manic individuals are not able to judge objectively their own rationality. They feel their self-centeredness is deserved because they are so special—something like a "bridezilla" who feels that being at the center of attention at all times is thoroughly legitimate. Depressive moods are seen in several mental illnesses, but the manic mood swing differentiates bipolar disease.

3. Bipolar disorder tends to involve episodes of completely normal function between mood swings.

With most mental illness, individuals retain some trace of their symptoms, or the symptoms disappear only gradually. For example, someone with severe panic attacks may still have twinges of anxiety in certain situations even when medication prevents the severe reactions they used to experience. But bipolar patients suddenly switch from a manic or depressive mood to a state that is totally normal— that is, to functioning with the same personality they had before the mood swing began. This characteristic was identified long before there were medication treatments to shorten the period of manic activity. In a true bipolar case, the mood swing can disappear as spontaneously and completely as it appeared, and the person will have no symptoms of mental illness for some period of time.

4. *Bipolar mood swings generally last for days or weeks (not hours).*

Most of the time, mood swings in bipolar patients are episodes that last an extended number of days, although treatment with medication now shortens the period from the weeks and weeks of mania that individuals endured in the past. Some individuals have what is called rapid cycling, but this is not common. Rapid cycling bipolar disorder is a term for individuals who have four or more mood swings within a year. The term rapid cycling should not be applied to explosive outbursts or mood shifts that come and go within a few hours.

5. *Bipolar mood swings come on unpredictably, not necessarily in response to a specific circumstance or event.*

A true bipolar mood swing seems to occur whimsically—without an obvious cause. A person may be functioning and feeling fine, and suddenly develop a depressive or manic mood swing. A loved one of the patient may say something like "I don't understand why this happened. Nothing has been going on to cause it." Bipolar swings are by definition spontaneous and arbitrary disturbances of mental and social function, not emotional reactions that accelerate into a loss of mental and physical control.

An example of a bipolar mood swing could be described by the following story: "George was fine on Sunday, and George was fine on Monday. On Tuesday, George confided to me that he was President Washington reincarnated and he's packing for his move into the White House."

In contrast, when Johnny is told he can't leave class to get a drink, and ends up in a violent meltdown swinging his fists, cursing, and spitting at his teacher—there is nothing in that chain of events that describes a manic mood swing. Johnny's behavior occurred in response to a social interaction.

PART II

INSTINCTS AND VIOLENT AGGRESSION

CHAPTER 3

Behavior Problems in Children Caused by Adrenaline System Over-Reactivity

❧

MOST people know there is adrenaline in their bodies, and they can feel its effects. People will say, "I had an adrenaline rush!" or "I was all pumped up on adrenaline." When we compete in sports or when our car swerves to a screeching stop just short of a collision, we have a heightened sense of mental alertness and physical stimulation brought on by an increased level of adrenaline. Those events are standard experiences in our culture.

What is less commonly understood is how intense an adrenaline response can be. For example, most people have not experienced an extreme, life- threatening situation—like fighting in a war zone—when adrenaline system reactivity can take control of a person's entire body and mind. Even less known is that two types of adrenaline reactivity exist—"beta" and "alpha."[8]

The beta adrenaline system is dominant when an individual is frightened and feels in danger. This is referred to as a "Fright/Flight" response. The alpha system is dominant when an individual is aggressive with a focused and controlled attack. This is referred to as a "Focus/Fight" response.

---

8. There are also two types of adrenaline hormones: epinephrine and norepinephrine. "Beta" crisis reactivity is driven by high epinephrine levels in the blood and "alpha" crisis reactivity is driven by high norepinephrine levels in the blood. This is discussed in more detail later.

Hope for the Violently Aggressive Child

The adrenaline component of aggressive behavior is mostly unrecognized, particularly in children. Because the relationship between excessive adrenaline activity and behavioral symptoms is not well understood, many medical and behavioral professionals conclude that children with episodes of uncontrollable aggression have an underlying mental illness. The role of adrenaline arousal is not even a consideration when most clinicians make a diagnosis for children who are seen for complaints of aggression, violent meltdowns, attacking, intense anger when told "no," swearing and threatening, etc.

However, as mentioned in Part I, children with immature adrenaline reflexes can have such intense surges of adrenaline that they lose control physically and mentally. They may react as if they are being chased or attacked by a bear, even though they are really inside their house or classroom.

Children can outgrow adrenaline system over-reactivity with medication treatment, time, and behavioral help. Adrenaline-acting medicines target the excess output of adrenaline that triggers the episode. The daily dose can be adjusted so that adrenaline over-reactivity is blocked only to the extent that the child can function with more rational control—which is to function more often like their normal personality.

The following examples introduce the two different adrenaline crisis reactions that are relevant to many children with episodic aggression: the "beta-adrenergic" rage reaction (relates to fear and avoiding danger), and the "alpha-adrenergic" rage reaction (relates to attacking and fighting threats). The two distinct states of adrenaline-driven rage reactions can be identified by the different behavioral and physical characteristics that they present.

CHAPTER 3

THE EXAMPLE OF "BETA BOB"—BETA-ADRENERGIC "FRIGHT/FLIGHT" RAGE

Let's imagine an 8-year-old boy named Bob, who has some compulsive tendencies like insisting that his books and toys be always stored in the same place. His school bus comes between 8:30 and 8:35 a.m. However, last Tuesday, it was delayed by road construction. At 8:35 a.m., Bob starts to say repetitively, "My school bus is late. My school bus is late." He begins getting upset and pacing around. His hands begin to shake slightly. Suddenly he hits himself on the shoulder, then hits the wall and shouts, "Where is the school bus?!" At this point, his father walks up, puts his arm around Bob's shoulders and says calmly but firmly: "Bob, I'm sorry the school bus is late. It will be here soon. You need to calm down. We'll wait for it together." Bob is then able to calm down and wait until the school bus arrives.

In this example, Bob has no mature, rational ability to handle the distress he feels when there is an unexpected change in his schedule. Bob gains security from having consistency in his routines. Unexpected events make him feel insecure and afraid. His fear triggered the release of epinephrine (a type of adrenaline) into his bloodstream, where it activated his beta adrenaline receptors, resulting in his heart rate becoming faster and his heart beat more forceful. He could feel his heart pound and his fingers tremor slightly from side to side. These physical sensations added to his mental distress and made Bob feel even more upset. So he hit himself and then the wall. When Bob's father hugged him, assured him, and said he would stay with him, Bob felt more secure and his adrenaline reaction toned down.

On another day, had a babysitter been at home instead of his father, Bob's agitation over the delayed bus might have progressed into a severe, violent beta-adrenergic rage reaction. He might have run down the street or around the yard yelling about the bus and repeatedly hitting himself and anything in his way. Some people refer to this situation as having a "violent meltdown". Without the comforting intervention of a loving authority like his father, Bob's adrenaline reactivity could have continued to spiral upward and out of control.

Bob's physical and behavioral symptoms characterize beta adrenaline system over-reactivity.

THE EXAMPLE OF "ALPHA ABBY"—ALPHA-ADRENERGIC "FOCUS/FIGHT" RAGE

We can also imagine a 10-year-old girl named Abby who lives with her grandmother. Abby is sitting in Sunday school at snack time when the boy behind her starts saying that he is going to steal her cookie. The third time he says this, she stands up, throws him to the ground, and yells, "You leave me alone and keep your *#@&*^ hands off my stuff!" The teacher intervenes, but Abby, with a threatening glare, screams, "Leave me alone! I'll kill you!" Abby's grandmother is called to the room. Grandma tells the teacher that Abby occasionally has outbursts, and no one should try to hold or touch her or she'll get even angrier. Finally, Grandma talks Abby into going to an empty room, where Abby yells and stomps around for ten minutes before she calms down. Afterwards, someone tells Grandma that Abby had been just fine that morning, until she suddenly "went crazy" and looked "as if she were possessed."

Abby's episode demonstrates an alpha-adrenergic rage reaction (this type of violent meltdown is sometimes called "crazy-eyed rage," "psychotic-looking rage," "blackout rage," or "predator rage"). This may be the

CHAPTER 3

most difficult type of aggressive episode to deal with, and it seems to be a primary cause for the increase in children receiving a diagnosis of bipolar disorder in recent years. During an episode, the child looks and acts so out of touch with reality that caregivers and physicians conclude that there must be mental disorder involved. Actually, Abby's "crazy-eyed rage" is rooted in a normal instinctive response to her feelings of being threatened. Her adrenaline over-reactivity is too extreme for the social environment, and the adults present do not under- stand where her intensity is coming from. It is coming from the feeling that others are intruding on her personal territory and trying to take away her personal control. Abby responded to the boy and to the Sunday school teacher as if they were threatening enemies whom she needed to attack. Her body's excessive alpha-adrenergic reactivity fueled the intense, focused, aggressive change in her behavior.

Abby's physical and behavioral symptoms characterize alpha adrenaline system over-reactivity.

The majority of us have never seen or heard of a child showing extreme violence unless the child was mentally ill or had experienced significant emotional trauma. Though everyone is born with these survival reflexes, most individuals do not demonstrate adrenaline-driven rage behavior past the age of two or three. People learn social restraint, gain more rational control, or develop alternate ways of expression through the intimate care of family and culture. For a variety of reasons, more children today are not developing mature control over these instinctive survival responses.

It may sound bizarre to state that the intense physical and mental changes generated by the crisis adrenaline reflexes are "natural." How can states of severe panic and aggression be useful to survival? Think of tribal teenagers living in a primitive village. In the middle of the day, a pack of wild dogs invades the village, trying to attack the weaker inhabitants. The teens run with the other children in panic from the predators, with the older ones climbing safely into trees. When the teens look down and see the younger children being attacked and bitten by dogs without any adults to defend them, their instincts may change from fear to a protector role. A surge of norepinephrine fills them with bravado, and they jump down and wildly charge the dogs—scaring the startled animals away with their sudden, intense aggressive challenge.

Some people might describe these teenagers as going berserk. The term "berserk" is derived from a tribe of Norsemen called the "Berserkers" who revved themselves up into an alpha-adrenergic frenzy before a battle.[9] Their wild-eyed rush produced extreme fear in their enemies, who knew the warriors would attack ferociously without any regard for their own lives. Some people claim the Berserkers used drugs to induce their ferocious state. This may or may not be true, but it is important to recognize that drugs are not necessary to induce psychotic-looking rage. The body's own natural chemicals can produce such a state.

While working in a rural clinic in Asia, I witnessed an amazing demonstration of how the adrenaline system can help the human body survive mortal danger. A man was brought to our clinic by his family, who had carried him on a board stretcher for over a mile. He was yelling continuously and loudly about his pain—a very unusual scene in that country, where people regularly tolerate extreme pain quietly.

I immediately went over to investigate. Out of habit I felt for his pulse as I began to examine him. There was no pulse! I looked down and saw that his arm was grey and lifeless. Quickly I put my stethoscope on his

---

9. http://en.wikipedia.org/wiki/Berserker

CHAPTER 3

chest and heard a loud, fast, churning heart beat. I then noticed his abdomen was also churning up and down. The man had had symptoms of cholera-like diarrhea for almost a full day, and he was severely dehydrated. His body had shut down all the circulation to his arms and legs so that what little blood and fluid he had left would be dedicated to fighting off the overwhelming infection in his abdomen!

At the time, I did not understand that it was through an alpha adrenergic "focus/fight" crisis response that his body had narrowed the blood vessels in his limbs. Had he instead had a "fright/flight" beta adrenergic reaction to his perilous situation, his blood vessels would have dilated and his remaining physical energy would not have been focused on attacking the invading bacteria in his gut. He would probably have died on the trip, before reaching the clinic with its supply of life-saving fluid.

CHAPTER 4

Instincts and Adrenaline Crisis

જી∾

INSTINCTS AND THE DEVELOPMENT
OF RATIONAL CONTROL

INSTINCTS are the natural and "immature" behavior patterns that govern until rational, mature control develops. Immaturity does not mean only "acting like a selfish brat." The term also can mean "not yet having developed full control," and that can mean "not able to make a rational choice." A baby's instinct to suckle allows the child to get nutrition until muscle development and teeth allow the more mature ability to chew. Despite being automatic responses, instincts can be quite complex and amazingly specific to particular species. For example, I have read that when a mother kangaroo is escaping a pursuing enemy (e.g., a dingo), at a certain point of tiredness, she will throw her baby joey out of the pouch. Instead of following its mother as one might expect, in this crisis situation the baby will instinctively start hopping in the opposite direction from the mother. The dingo then has the difficult decision of chasing a smaller prey who is not tired, or pursuing the mother who is no longer carrying the weight of a passenger.

Some children with adrenaline-driven behavior problems, especially the beta type, will apologize afterwards saying they knew better and tried to stop themselves but could not. Parents at first may doubt the sincerity of the apologies, but over time may recognize the child's apologies as genuine. In many cases, children are truly anguished that they cannot obey and "behave" when they are under an intense adrenaline surge. In my experience, such children gain so much more rational control when taking an adrenaline-acting medicine that the children themselves may be the first to object if someone suggests they go off of the medicine.

INSTINCTS AND VIOLENCE

Some people question whether young children have a natural capacity for violence. There is a belief, almost a superstition, that newborns are innocent and unspoiled until they learn otherwise. There is little evidence for this idea in the natural world.

Consider the case of twelve piglets whose mother has only eleven nipples. As the piglets struggle against each other to get some of mother's milk, the largest or most aggressive eleven eventually will prevent one from getting any nutrition. Finally the runt will starve. Its brothers or sisters were never deliberately violent against it, but they instinctively shoved it aside in their own pursuit of food. Similarly, if you observe two-year-old toddlers in a daycare class you will see them grab what they want, push, bite, and hit others in their way. Only with constant intervention of caregivers do toddlers learn other strategies.

ADRENALINE SYSTEM OVER-REACTIVITY AND VIOLENCE

Instinctive violence is an inborn, self-preserving, survival reaction that has been misunderstood in children, and has been frequently misdiagnosed as various mental disorders—especially bipolar disorder.

CHAPTER 4

Excessive adrenaline reactivity causes not only aggressive behavior, but also physical symptoms that can be observed by measuring specific changes in heart rate, blood pressure, and skin color. When a child has a meltdown, the adrenaline systems are overactive. Physicians and parents will spend years trying various medications and behavior plans to deal with an aggressive child and never consider monitoring the child's blood pressure and heart rate to observe how extreme the child's physical reactivity is during the episodes.

For example, Beta Bob had a beta-adrenergic reaction when his school bus was late. The term "beta-adrenergic" means the stimulation of the beta adrenaline receptors is the dominant reaction. Because of Bob's anxious, compulsive personality, he likely would have had a somewhat high heart rate such as 86 beats per minute, even when not upset. When Bob began obsessing about the late school bus and got physically agitated, the beta adrenaline arousal would cause an increase in blood flow and his heart rate would likely go over 120 beats per minute, his blood pressure to 140/70.[10] His face might become visibly flushed.

Another physical sign of Bob's beta adrenaline over-reactivity was the side-to-side tremor of his fingers when he was distraught. Children who have frequent beta "fright" over-arousal often pick or bite their fingernails or cuticles. In order for Bob to have stability, the adrenaline over-reactivity he develops when he is frightened or anxious needs to be addressed directly.

Signs and symptoms that point to beta adrenaline system over-arousal include the following:

---

10. In beta-adrenergic arousal, the top number of the blood pressure becomes higher than normal because of the force and increased speed of the heart rate. The bottom number drops lower than normal since the blood vessels are dilated (wider) and can hold more blood.

- The child has explosions of sudden anger when frustrated.
- The child strikes out in an unfocused and random way.
- The child's face or body becomes flushed (reddens).
- After episodes, the child apologizes or says that he/she tried to stop but could not.
- The child's anger reaction may be calmed quickly by certain authority figures with physical or verbal intervention.
- The child's heart beats fast or "pounds" during the episode.
- The child's hands or fingers tremor (shake slightly).
- The child bites or picks at fingernails or skin.
- The child exhibits unusual strength during episodes.
- The child shows high physical activity as part of normal personality (i.e., rarely sits still for very long even while watching television).
- The child has a high resting heart rate (90 beats per minute or above).

Treatment plans that do not take those physical symptoms into account are not likely to be effective.

On the other hand, Alpha Abby's adrenaline-driven "alpha" rage reaction presents different physical signs. Her heart rate and blood pressure when she was sitting in the Sunday school class before snack time were within normal ranges. Once the boy made her angry about the cookie, her alpha adrenaline system arousal reduced her blood flow (constricted her blood vessels), making her face paler (instead of flushed) and her blood pressure very high—perhaps as high as 160/100.[11] Her heart rate became faster than normal also, but not nearly as high as Beta Bob's. Another

---

11. In alpha-adrenergic arousal, the top and bottom numbers of the blood pressure become higher than normal because of the constriction (narrowing) of the blood vessels.

physical sign of Abby's alpha adrenaline system over-reactivity is her "crazy" or "evil"-looking, glazed eyes.

Signs and symptoms that point to alpha-adrenergic over-arousal include the following:

- The child's personality changes during rage episodes (i.e., becoming hateful with swearing).
- The child threatens to kill or harm others during rages.
- After rages the child does not seem remorseful.
- The child denies or does not remember certain events of the rage.
- The child becomes more violent if there is any attempt to hold or restrain during a rage.
- The child's aggression seems deliberate and targeted.
- The child's eyes have a "crazy" or "evil" look during rages.
- The child's blood pressure is >15 points higher than usual during rages (both numbers).
- The child's face and extremities may get pale during rages.

DIAGRAM: THE TWO TYPES OF ADRENALINE AROUSAL

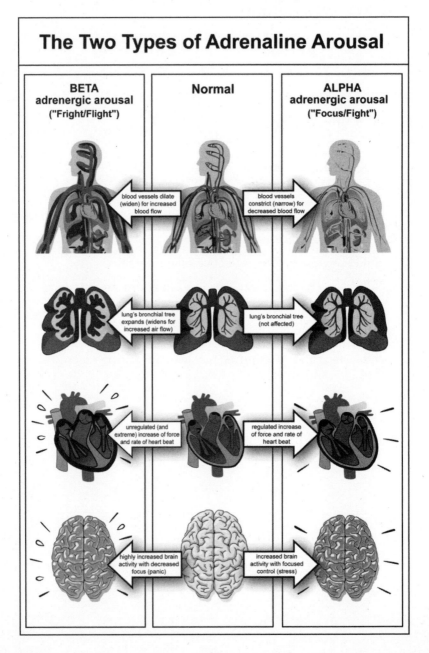

CHAPTER 4

BEHAVIOR MANAGEMENT CONSIDERATIONS FOR
A CHILD WITH VIOLENT AGGRESSION

If a child in your care has violent meltdowns, you might consider the following strategies to see if any are helpful in reducing the length or intensity of the episodes:

- Focus on whether the child is doing right, instead of focusing on the attitude they are having.
- Phrase requests in a way that gives the child more control over the answer (For example, "Your room needs cleaning today, when can you get to that?" instead of "Go clean up your room, it's a mess.").
- When a meltdown does occur, only one person should be in charge of dealing with the child, and that person should not be personally upset.
- If person A is not having much success dealing with the child, switch to person B. Do not have multiple authority figures talking at the child at once.
- During meltdowns, be prepared to ignore and disregard the foul language and hurtful statements that may come out of the child's mouth.
- Do not ask the child, "Why do you act that way?"
- Set definite rules for any discussions about the child's episodes. For example: a) they are discussed only one time with the child (or only one time with each parent); b) when they are discussed with a physician, the child is (or is not) present; c) discussions can occur only with a child who is sufficiently calm. In some cases, the best rule might be that there will be no discussions at all (if all discussions lead to more negative interactions).

- Do not promise the child that you will keep the child's behavior secret. That said; avoid public discussions with friends or family about the child's episodes.
- When giving consequences, verbalize them in advance whenever possible. For example, before turning off the child's computer, say, "Since you did not clean your room, your computer will be turned off (or taken out of the room)."

The next chapter is written to provide an overview of the reactivity of the separate adrenaline systems. Although more technical, it is important to address these basic physiological issues, since treatments based on this information are unfamiliar to the majority of behavioral practitioners. I hope to provide sufficient detail and background to demonstrate why it is reasonable to prescribe adrenaline-acting medications instead of "psychiatric" medications to treat certain types of aggressive episodes.

CHAPTER 5

Two Systems of
Adrenaline Reactivity

❧

HOW THE TWO ADRENALINE SYSTEMS WORK

EPINEPHRINE AND NOREPINEPHRINE:
THE TWO ADRENALINE HORMONES

HERE are two chemicals in the body that belong to the adrenaline family: epinephrine and norepinephrine. Both are made in the adrenal gland near the kidney. Norepinephrine is also made in certain specialized nerve cells.

Adrenaline activity in the body involves both epinephrine and norepinephrine. Epinephrine is circulated through the body only through the circulatory system (arteries and veins). Norepinephrine is also circulated through the blood system, but additionally it can be released by the sympathetic nervous system. (This system is the way the brain communicates with involuntary functions of the body. For example, when a person stands up, the brain tells the blood vessels in the legs to constrict. This action prevents blood from pooling in the legs, which would make the person pass out. The brain is constantly sending these kinds of messages to adjust involuntary systems in the body in reaction to environmental changes of movement, temperature, exertion, etc.)

Hope for the Violently Aggressive Child

Epinephrine and norepinephrine are the chemicals that together act on adrenaline receptors to cause the reactions referred to as "adrenaline reactivity." The various interactions between those two chemicals and the body's alpha- and beta-receptors produce the various states of "adrenaline over-reactivity" that can lead to the aggressive behavior referred to here as "adrenergic rage reactions."

Norepinephrine would seem to be the more important hormone in the first reaction to an environmental crisis. When there is a crisis, norepinephrine is quickly secreted through two extensive nerve networks, the sympathetic system in the body and the locus ceruleus portion of the brain. Also, nerve fibers from these systems instantly release norepinephrine to the body's vital organs, causing constriction (narrowing) in muscles and blood vessels. This survival mechanism helps prevent excessive blood loss when the body is wounded.

Depending on the nature of the threat and the experience of the individual, the hormones released from the adrenal gland will change the individual's physical dynamics in one of two directions: to flee from the danger or to attack it. This is accomplished by the variation in the percentage of norepinephrine as opposed to epinephrine released into the blood stream.

If more norepinephrine than epinephrine is released, this indicates the individual has determined to fight or to try to control the situation. The norepinephrine arousal produces a focused tension needed for hunters and warriors to carry out aggressive activities.

If there is considerably more epinephrine than norepinephrine released, this indicates the individual is frightened of the perceived danger, and the body is gearing up to run away. Epinephrine is the hormone that supports vigorous muscular exertion. This is accomplished by its particular

CHAPTER 5

property of dilating (expanding) the blood vessels, which supplies more nutrition and oxygen than usual to the muscle so that it can function at maximum capacity.

Predators like lions run high levels of norepinephrine, and prey animals such as antelopes run exceptionally high levels of epinephrine.[12] Research has been done showing that the human epinephrine and norepinephrine ratio is more variable according to the situation, but in crisis situations, the tendency is for humans to react with a fear response and the secretion of a high ratio of epinephrine.

BETA AND ALPHA ADRENALINE RECEPTORS

The way that the body responds to the presence of epinephrine and norepinephrine is through special structures called adrenaline receptors. Adrenaline receptors are located in the cell walls of nerves and organs throughout the body. The receptors signal the body's organs and tissues to react depending on the amount of either epinephrine or norepinephrine they detect.

The system of adrenaline receptors is complex. There are beta adrenaline receptors and alpha adrenaline receptors. The two classes are based on similarities in structure, not similarities in function. There also are subtypes of beta and alpha receptors.

In most of the body, alpha receptors are stimulated by norepinephrine, and beta receptors are stimulated by epinephrine. In certain organs (the brain and heart), the beta receptors respond to both epinephrine and norepinephrine. In these areas, alpha receptors are less significant.

---

12. Goodall, McC. "Studies of adrenaline and noradrenaline in mammalian heart and suprarenals." Acta Physiol Scand Suppl. 1951;24(85):7-51.

Hope for the Violently Aggressive Child

Today most physicians are aware that alpha and beta receptors are different, particularly in the context that different kinds of medicines will act on each receptor type with differing effect. What is not well understood are the complexities of how the two systems of adrenaline affect behavior. Nor is there a strong understanding of the roles of epinephrine and norepinephrine in stimulating the alpha and beta receptors to generate different physical states of adrenaline arousal.

Both types of adrenaline receptors act in the body and the brain, but not in the same way in each area. For purposes of illustration, I refer to the "alpha- adrenergic system" and the "beta-adrenergic system" as if the two receptor systems were anatomically separate. Such a separation is simplistic from a scientific perspective, but important to explain key distinctions between the behavioral and physical responses when the reactivity of one system is dominant over the other.

DIFFERENCES IN STRUCTURE AND FUNCTION BETWEEN THE BETA- AND ALPHA-ADRENERGIC SYSTEMS:

Adrenaline Receptors in the Body

The clearest difference between the beta- and alpha-adrenergic systems is apparent through the opposite effect each system has on the tubular, involuntary muscles that make up the vital organs of the body (e.g. the blood vessels and intestines). When these involuntary muscles are activated by beta receptors, the way they respond is nearly opposite to how they respond when activated by alpha receptors.

Beta adrenaline receptors in the body's involuntary muscles are called "beta-2" receptors. When stimulated by epinephrine, these receptors

CHAPTER 5

cause the muscles of the tubular organs to relax and the diameter of the muscles to widen (dilation). Beta-2 receptors are not stimulated by norepinephrine, and they do not have significant function in the heart and brain. The primary purposes for beta-2 receptor activity seem to involve preparing the body for high physical activity in times of stress by dilating the blood vessels and lungs, reducing the activity of other organs such as the intestines, and regulating the release of sugar (glucose) into the blood stream.

The principle alpha adrenaline receptors located in the blood vessels and intestines are called "alpha-1" receptors. When stimulated by norepinephrine, the receptors cause the muscles to constrict and the diameter of the muscles to narrow. Alpha-1 receptors are not stimulated by epinephrine in a way that is important to crisis reactivity.

Thus, in the involuntary muscles of the body's vital organs, there are opposing actions that offset each other. One type of adrenaline (epinephrine) stimulates a "beta-adrenergic" response of muscle relaxation through the beta-2 receptors. The other adrenaline hormone, norepinephrine, stimulates an "alpha-adrenergic" response of muscle contraction through the alpha-1 receptors.

Adrenaline Receptors in the Heart

In the heart, the beta receptors respond differently. In the heart, both epinephrine and norepinephrine stimulate the same beta receptor, called the "beta-1" receptor.[13] When this receptor is stimulated, the heart rate increases and the beat of the heart is more forceful. This action increases

---

13. Note that although there are receptors named "beta-1" and "beta-2," as well as "alpha-1" and "alpha-2," they were named by different scientists. Thus, the meaning of the "1" and the "2" are not consistent in terms of function.

the volume and the pressure of the blood flow. In crisis situations, this increase of blood flow is needed to increase physical and mental activity.

Alpha-1 adrenaline receptors are present in the heart muscle, but their activity is not significant to crisis adrenaline reactions.

ADRENALINE RECEPTORS IN THE BRAIN

In the brain, norepinephrine stimulates beta-1 receptors, just like in the heart, but the norepinephrine that activates the brain comes exclusively from nerve fibers within the brain. Epinephrine and norepinephrine circulating in the body's blood stream are prevented from entering the brain by a network called the "blood brain barrier."[14] Thus, norepinephrine is the major adrenaline-acting chemical in the brain, and most of the brain's adrenaline receptors are beta-1 receptors.

Because there is significantly more beta than alpha activity directly influencing the brain cells, it may be that the alpha-adrenergic rage state is not caused by direct alpha stimulation to nerve cells of the brain, but instead to alpha stimulation of the blood vessels supplying the brain. Recent successful clinical experiences treating formerly intractable cases of rage behavior with the new beta-blocker Bystolic is most readily attributed to Bystolic's unique maintenance of blood vessel vasodilatation. (Bystolic is a registered trade name. The generic name is nebivolol.) Other beta-blockers have some vaso-constrictive effect, which in some cases could have been the cause of beta adrenaline reactivity moving into an alpha-adrenergic rage reaction.

---

14. The blood brain barrier is the membrane or chemical "fence" that keeps much of the contents of the blood and other tissues from penetrating and disturbing the brain's fine-tuned activities.

CHAPTER 5

AN ILLUSTRATION OF ADRENALINE SYSTEM ACTIVITY: "THE CRUISE SHIP" MODEL

Because it is not easy to understand all the different parts of the adrenaline system, I offer the following story as an illustration. After all, people tend to remember the details of a vacation trip longer than they remember things they read in a book.

Picture a cruise ship named "Excitement" docked off the coast of an island. The island represents a person's body in a normal state, and it has three casinos: the Brain Casino, the Heart Casino, and the Vital Organs Casino (vital organs consist of the lungs, digestive system, urinary and reproductive systems).

The ship "Excitement" is full of passengers who represent adrenaline hormones. Some of the passengers are norepinephrine types (NEs), professional gamblers who are experienced, disciplined, and focused in their approach to gaming. Other passengers are epinephrine types (EPIs), casual vacationers who want to have fun in the middle of a crowd where there is a lot of activity and movement. Once the ship is moored, the passengers debark and surge out to stir up some action at the casinos.

When the vacationer EPIs (epinephrine) and gambler NEs (norepinephrine) stream into the Vital Organs Casino, the different types of passengers are kept separate from each other.

The EPIs (vacationers) go into large rooms designed for noisy fun with lots of space for onlookers to mill around. These rooms represent the body's beta-2 receptors which are plentiful in the vital organs. The beta-2 receptors attract and hold epinephrine— but not norepinephrine. When enough EPIs hit the beta-2 "tables," signals are sent to the muscles of the nearby organs to dilate and make more room (increase the size of the opening of the various tubular structures in the vital organs). A person experiencing this mild level of EPI excitement may have flushed warm skin, slightly shaking hands, and deeper breathing.

CHAPTER 5

If too many EPIs (vacationers) pack into the casino, the crowd can become panicky. Instead of a fun party atmosphere, the interaction becomes upset and agitated and the EPIs lose rational control. Now they just want to GET OUT of the casino, and they may push and fight and trample each other while they attempt to do so. This situation represents the beta crisis adrenaline state or "beta rage reaction".

NEs (gamblers) at the Vital Organs Casino have no interest in the party rooms where the EPIs (vacationers) go. Instead, the NEs are attracted to narrow, quiet rooms with efficient sparse furnishings where activity is limited to the game table. These rooms represent the alpha-1 receptors, which are also located in abundance in the Vital Organs Casino. In these rooms, the number of NEs who can sit at the table is limited and there is no place for an audience. This rule is so strict that there are special areas where NEs must wait until their scheduled time to play. These special waiting rooms are like the alpha-2 receptors. (Norepinephrine stimulates alpha-2 and alpha-1 receptors at the same time, and the main action of the alpha-2 receptors is to regulate the release of norepinephrine to the alpha-1 receptors.)

Hope for the Violently Aggressive Child

When lots of NEs (gamblers) stream into the alpha rooms, the receptors signal the muscles of the nearby organs to constrict and make less room (decrease the size of the opening of the various tubular structures in the vital organs). The person experiencing this mild level of NE excitement might feel some tightness in swallowing, a queasy feeling in the abdomen, and cool or numb hands.

If too many NEs (gamblers) pack into the casino, the waiting rooms can't hold the players back. The orderly professional gambling environment is lost and the NE players, who generally are so controlled, now begin to turn on one other in a focused, threatening, and attacking way. Nobody is willing to back down, so they pull out knives and go for each other's throats. This situation represents the very dangerous alpha crisis adrenaline state or "alpha rage reaction." It tends to be more dangerous than the beta rage reaction, because there is more ability for a person's intellect to plan and direct an attack, and less ability for the intellect to feel that the violent activities are wrong.

The Heart Casino has a different arrangement, with most of its space dedicated to gaming rooms with beta-1 tables, which represent the beta-1 adrenaline receptors in the heart muscle. The rooms have the same size and social atmosphere of the beta-2 rooms back at the Vital Organs Casino, but with a big difference: at the Heart Casino, both type of passengers play at the same table. EPIs and NEs are both attracted to beta-1 receptors. If more NEs are at the table, the receptor will send a message to the heart muscle to increase heart activity with focused regulation. If EPIs are crowding all the beta-1 tables, the heart muscle will have a highly unregulated increase in heart activity.

CHAPTER 5

During a beta crisis adrenaline state (EPI arousal), a person may have a "weird feeling" in the heart due to an unregulated, racing heart rate. During an alpha crisis adrenaline state (NE arousal), the person may have a "weird feeling" that their heart is pounding in their chest— caused by the increased force required to pump enough blood through their narrowed blood vessels.

The Brain Casino is listed last because its situation is extremely unique. EPIs generally do not go there! The brain is also unusual in that most of the important adrenaline activity occurs through the NEs playing at rooms with beta-1 tables. Thus, like in the Heart Casino, the brain can be aroused in either a highly regulated or highly unregulated way.

CHAPTER 6

Two Adrenaline Crisis States

꙰

T HE relevance of alpha versus beta adrenaline activity on the body's vital organs is well illustrated by the adrenaline crisis states found in a scene of the hunter and the hunted.

EXAMPLES OF ADRENALINE CRISIS STATES IN THE ANIMAL WORLD

The Hunted: The Physical Symptoms of Beta Adrenaline Activation

When an essentially defenseless rabbit is startled by the sudden attack of a predator, it depends on an extreme state of beta-adrenergic over-arousal to survive. The sole function of the rabbit is to escape. Its instinctive panic causes a surge of epinephrine to be released. Beta-2 receptors are stimulated, and the vital organ's involuntary muscles widen, allowing an increase of blood volume in the blood vessels and increased airflow in the lungs. Those changes, along with a more forceful and fast heart rate, gives the rabbit maximum physical ability to run as fast and far as possible.

At the same time, the beta response in the rabbit's brain produces a mental state with little rational focus. The fleeing animal may crash head-long through barbed wire without hesitation. The fleeing rabbit demonstrates the fright/ flight beta adrenaline crisis state.

If eventually cornered or trapped, the rabbit may turn on the predator in a frenzied state—kicking and biting the attacker with unusual strength until it either dies or breaks free to run away again.

Hope for the Violently Aggressive Child

The rabbit does not have controlled reactions to the environment during the beta-adrenergic flight/fright crisis state. It may severely injure itself in ways it normally would avoid, and the "last-resort" fighting is frenzied rather than strategic. However, this response is an effective survival mechanism for an animal with reasonable odds of recovering from minor injuries and no chance of surviving capture.

The Hunter: The Physical Symptoms of Alpha Adrenaline Activation

The predator in the scene above is not in a state of mindless, beta-adrenergic panic like its rabbit prey. In order to get close enough to spring before the rabbit takes off running, the stalking predator is in an alpha-adrenergic state of focused, controlled tension (often described by humans as "stress").

The alpha receptors are stimulated by norepinephrine, which is released to support the stalking behavior by narrowing the blood vessels and increasing the muscular tension in the limbs. Even the predator's heart rate can be modulated during this state of disciplined agitation. With great focus and control, the predator slowly, carefully, and deliberately creeps up on its prey. This demonstrates the "focus" aspect of the alpha-adrenergic focus/fight arousal. If the predator catches its prey, it will violently attack and kill it. This demonstrates the attacking, "fight" characteristic of the alpha-adrenergic crisis arousal state.

Watching films of a lion unsuccessfully chasing an antelope, viewers may think the lion "gives up" too quickly, but the predator is better off stalking a new meal rather than losing a meal in a prolonged chase. The predator is under severe physical stress, and its constricted blood vessels cannot produce the energy to run at full speed for very long.

CHAPTER 6

The increased force of the pumping heart in these two different states of adrenergic crisis produces high blood pressure. In the rabbit where blood vessels are widened (dilated) by beta-adrenergic reactivity, the bottom number would be lower than normal (e.g., 150/60). This allows the maximum amount of blood to flow through the rabbit's muscles so it has the energy to run on and on even though the heart is beating hard. In the predator, where the blood vessels are narrowed (constricted) by alpha-adrenergic reactivity, both blood pressure numbers would be elevated (e.g., 170/110). Thus, the predator cannot continue intense physical exertion for a long time because not enough blood can move through its constricted blood vessels to provide sustained energy.

THE PHYSIOLOGY OF ADRENALINE
CRISIS STATES IN HUMANS

Humans demonstrate both prey and predator behavior, and the human adrenaline system can emphasize beta- or alpha-adrenergic crisis reactivity. In general, the initial startle response in humans to a potential danger involves beta receptor activity. (Most people consider this startle reactivity to be the "flight/fight" reaction. I understand it as the first phase of a more intricate system of adrenaline activity.) The important organs of this initial response are the heart and the brain, which are aroused through the beta-1 receptors. These receptors are stimulated by norepinephrine.

In the relatively safe and civilized society of America, most initial "primitive" adrenaline reactions calm down immediately after the person realizes that there is no severe danger. If a life-threatening crisis does exist, or if the person (or child) perceives that such a threat exists, the adrenaline reactivity will develop into a full crisis response in one of two directions. The crisis response will be either a "beta system" crisis state stimulated by epinephrine or an "alpha system" crisis state stimulated by norepinephrine.

For individuals who develop adrenergic rage reactions, what is significant is the adrenaline reactivity that occurs after the initial "primitive" startle response. In the following histories, individual cases of adrenaline system over-arousal are described, as well as the medication therapies and behavioral controls I used for treatment.

PART III

CASE STUDIES AND CLINICAL EXPERIENCES

CHAPTER 7

Adrenaline and Behavioral Science: Case Studies and Medical Literature

༄ ༅

I N my first years of practice as a psychiatrist, I saw patients whose therapeutic response to adrenaline-acting medicines was very rapid or unexpectedly effective. I also saw patients who did not show such improvements. I sought to discover why patients with seemingly similar symptoms of aggression or agitation did not have the same responses to the medicine. These experiences provided clues that pointed to the nature of the various interactions between adrenaline activity and the brain. Applying theoretical foundations to more cases through the years proved that greater predictability and success in treatment was possible.

The following case histories are presented in chronological order to help demonstrate my progress in clinical understanding over time, along with citations to the limited published literature I was able to find over the years relevant to this subject.

CASE #1: TREATMENT OF BETA-ADRENERGIC RAGE REACTION CAUSED BY BRAIN INJURY (EARLY 1980s):

Shortly after I began my psychiatric practice in the early 1980s, I was asked to evaluate the teenage son of a local businessman. The young man had sustained a brain injury in an automobile accident and since then suffered violent rages three to four times a day. His episodes involved shouting, threatening, and random physical violence. He was living in a nursing home, and he was too unstable to visit his parent's house.

This type of rage reaction had long been identified as a possible symptom following brain injury. It also was known not to respond to standard psychiatric medications (antipsychotics and mood stabilizers). I saw the patient only one time, and I recommended that he start propranolol 10 mgs twice a day. A year later, I was surprised to receive a letter of appreciation from his parents. The nursing home physician had read my recommendation and started their son on the beta-blocker.

Their son had not had violent rages since starting on propranolol. He was no longer as irritable in day-to-day interactions, and he was able to visit home regularly without difficulties.

COMMENT: In this consultation, I had recommended the use of propranolol because I was aware that in 1977, there was a paper by Dr. Frank Elliott demonstrating that propranolol greatly improved rage behavior in brain-injured patients.[17] This particular study involved a group of adults who had had normal function, sustained a brain trauma, and then began having random rage reactions. The episodes would come on suddenly, would be caused by minor situations, and would leave the individuals apologetic and confused about why they had become so upset.

This paper was unique among the literature about beta-blockers' effect on behavior. It was distinguished by having patients all of a definable group, with the same diagnosis and similar symptoms of aggression. The

---

17. Elliott F.A. "Propranolol for the control of belligerent behavior following acute brain damage." Ann Neurol, 1977; 1:489-491.

paper demonstrated three facts about rage in brain-injured individuals, which remain relevant today for treatment of rage:

1. That the rage symptoms of the brain-injured patients in the study were very similar, despite wide variation in the cause of their brain injuries;
2. In those who responded to beta-blocking medication, the response was rapid; and
3. The phenomenon of this type of rage was reversible in some patients, as evidenced by fifty percent of the patients in the study being able, over time, to discontinue their beta-blocking medications without recurrence of the rages.

At the time I saw the teenager in Case #1, I believed that the "brain injury rage" was a unique type of rage seen only in brain-injured patients.

I now understand that the sudden outburst of emotionally violent, spontaneous rages seen in many brain-injured individuals is caused by beta-adrenergic over-reactivity. It is brought on by a loss of control over the instinctive beta adrenaline responses as a consequence of the brain trauma. Once beta-blocking medicine helped this teenager control his excessive epinephrine reactivity, he regained the more mature control he had prior to the injury, and the rage episodes disappeared.

CASE #2: BENEFITS OF BETA-BLOCKING MEDICINES FOR PHYSICAL SYMPTOMS OF ANXIETY (1980s):

The following self-report was written at my request in the 1980s by an adult man I treated with a beta-blocker for symptoms of intense anxiety:

May 1983: "Propranolol has helped me by lowering my heart rate, which was unusually high during rest and non-physical activity. In lowering the rate it has seemed to have relieved the anxious feeling like I was racing on the inside—trying to deal with certain situations, but I could not think straight: frozen, just sitting there shaking. (I had) feelings of worthlessness and inadequacy. The lower heart rate seems to allow me to handle more normal situations that were almost impossible for me to handle before.

"It has helped me deal with some basic emotional growth. For instance, the days when I feel good about myself are greater than the ones when I feel bad. The bad ones are rare. I now have enough self confidence to realize that it's just one bad day or hour, and it's not the end of the world like I would have felt before.

"Now, as a result, I find I can go through life where I am more or less in control of my emotions, fears, feelings of worthlessness, denial, etc. rather than them being in control of me."

COMMENT: This man came to me with longstanding symptoms of anxiety, which had not responded adequately to anti-anxiety medicines like Valium. His chief complaints were the physical changes he felt when he was anxious, such as a racing heart and involuntary shaking. In a textbook I used during my psychiatric residency, I found the following statement that the beta-adrenergic blocker propranolol (trade name Inderal) was useful in anxiety:

"... Anxiety is characterized by palpitations, rapid heartbeat, tremor, tingling, cold sweats, chest constriction, and twitching. Physiologically,

---

18. Freedman, A.M., Kaplan, H.I., and Sadock, B.J. Modern Synopsis of Psychiatry: 2nd ed. Williams & Wilkins Co: Baltimore, 1976. Page 982.

CHAPTER 7

many of these symptoms can be caused by epinephrine secreted during stress. This point raises the question of whether one of the components in anxiety is the perception of these internal epinephrine-induced physiological events or even a hyper-awareness of normal adrenergic functioning. Many of these peripheral autonomic events can be blocked by β-adrenergic blocking agents, such as propranolol (Inderal)."

"The hypothesis here is that the β-adrenergic agent may block the autonomic signals of anxiety and, thus, may benefit anxiety through a peripheral mechanism. Propranolol, given either intravenously or orally in beta-receptor-blocking doses, produces improvements in patients with anxiety, particularly improvements in the somatic manifestations of anxiety."

"The use of β-blockers for anxiety is still in the investigation stage and is mentioned here for its theoretical relevance ..."[18]

A number of doctors and researchers in the 1970s and 1980s used beta- blockers to relieve the physical symptoms that intensified a patient's feelings of anxiety. A speaker at the 1985 American Psychiatric Association annual convention, Dr. Ferris Pitts, a professor of psychiatry at USC, challenged the audience by stating, "psychiatrists treat anxiety with benzodiazepines (tranquilizers), but family doctors treat anxiety with beta-blockers."[19]

Though beta-blockers relieve the physical symptoms that can accompany anxiety, alone they do not relieve the mental pressure that anxiety patients suffer. Thus, when the new serotonin antidepressant medications were shown to significantly reduce the mental symptoms of anxiety, beta-

---

19. Pitts, Ferris. "Beta-blockers and their utility." Symposium 9D. APA Annual Mtg: New York, 1985.

blockers no longer were considered a useful option for anxiety treatment, even for those cases where the relief of physical symptoms (racing heart, finger tremor, biting and picking fingernails) would give greater therapeutic relief than medication addressing the mental anxiety symptoms alone.

CASE #3: BENEFITS OF BETA-BLOCKING
MEDICINES FOR A HYPERACTIVE CHILD (1980s):

An 8-year-old girl was brought to me in the 1980s because she had pulled out all the hair from her head. She could not sit still for more than a few minutes at a time, so she was unable to function well at school. Several trials of stimulant medications for attention deficit hyperactivity disorder (ADHD) had failed. In order to handle her excessive activity, her mother had put her into three structured programs every afternoon after school. Her mother said the programs helped "wear her out enough" to go to sleep at night.

At her appointment, her heart rate was over 120 beats per minute while sitting! I placed her on propranolol, which lowered her resting heart rate to the 80/minute range. Her over-activity diminished considerably. She was able to grow her hair out. Additionally, she was able to stay in the regular class at school and no longer required the extreme schedule of after-school programming to sleep at night. In a letter her mother sent to me in 1983, she wrote:

"When I asked her how she feels since taking the medicine, she pointed to her chest and stomach and said 'I have peace, right here.' Her piano teacher told me that she has been especially sweet of late, very cooperative, and that her concentration is much improved. She said they worked together for an hour and she could easily go two hours with her now. There is no comparison as to how this child was before going on propranolol and how she is now."

Over the course of the next four years, this child was maintained on between 40 and 120 mgs propranolol per day (the dosage would be raised when she started to exhibit breakthrough symptoms like pulling hair, or lowered if her energy level seemed too low).

COMMENT: A physical result of beta-blocker therapy is a lower heart rate. So when I began prescribing beta-blockers for patients in the 1980s, I would always track their heart rates. In time, I expanded this practice and began tracking the heart rates of all of my patients. I discovered that certain of my "hyperactive" pediatric patients who had failed trials of ADHD stimulant medications ran exceptionally high heart rates all the time. They also had physical symptoms that I now recognize as being caused by excessive beta-adrenergic tone, such as finger tremor, biting fingernails or picking at skin, an inability to sit still, and an unusually high level of energy.

During these years, clinicians began "trying" propranolol to treat a variety of intractable symptoms including agitation, rage and violence, anxiety, and schizophrenia. The doctors communicated with each other and attended forums discussing each other's findings. Many well-respected and nationally known psychiatrists published an article or two on the potential therapeutic uses of beta-blockers.[20]

The trials that were done varied widely and produced mixed results:

Hope for the Violently Aggressive Child

1. Most positive studies saw results within a week or two, but one study showed no benefit until after 2-3 months of treatment.
2. Most studies used the beta-blocker propranolol, since its fat-solubility allowed it to enter the brain easily. One researcher, though, used the water-soluble beta-blocker nadolol, stating its therapeutic effect was in calming the "anxiety signals" of muscle tension, tremor, and rapid heart rate that the body sent to the brain.
3. No studies showed beta-blockers to be predictably effective for "aggression" or "agitation."

In the meantime, two new classes of powerful psychiatric medications were reaching the market: the serotonin-active antidepressants (SSRIs), and the "atypical" antipsychotics. As researchers began publishing studies demonstrating the wide scope of therapeutic benefits of these new medicines, interest in researching the benefits of beta-blockers diminished.

Interestingly, four specific "minor" disorders were found to be treated best by beta-blockers: a) performance anxiety—the use of low-dose propranolol immediately before a performance or presentation to calm the physical tremor in the voice and body; b) familial or "essential" tremor—

---

20. A sampling of literature during this period:

Suzman, M.M. "The use of β-adrenergic blockade with propranolol in anxiety symptoms."Postgrad Med J. 1971; 47:102-107.

Jefferson J.W. "Beta-adrenergic receptor blocking drugs in psychiatry." Arch Gen Psychiatry. 1974 Nov; 31(5):681-91.

Yudofsky S., Williams D.T., Gorman, J. "Propranolol in the treatment of rage and violent behavior in patients with chronic brain syndromes." Am J Psych, 1981; 138:218-220.

Williams D.T., Mehl R., Yudofsky S., et al: "The effect of propranolol on uncontrolled rage outbursts in children and adolescents with organic brain dysfunction." J Am Acad Child Psych, 1982; 21:120-135.

Sorgi P.J., Ratey J.J., Polakoff S. "Beta-adrenergic blockers for the control of aggressive behaviors in patients with chronic schizophrenia." Am J Psychiatry. 1986 Jun; 143(6):775-6.

CHAPTER 7

a hereditary disorder that causes a shaking tremor of the hands and sometimes the head (a well- known example was the actress Katharine Hepburn); c) treatment of tremor disorder caused as a side effect from lithium therapy; and d) treatment of akathisia, which is a movement side effect of antipsychotic medications.

CASE #4: DISCOVERY THAT TREATMENT OF RAGE BEHAVIOR WITH A BETA-BLOCKER CAN CAUSE IMPROVEMENT OF OTHER PSYCHIATRIC SYMPTOMS (1980s)

I evaluated a 22-year-old male patient with developmental disability and obsessive-compulsive traits. His major "maladaptive" behavior was an obsessive-compulsive drive to shake people's hands. If someone refused to shake his hand, he could develop intense, explosive rages and sometimes hit the person. Afterwards, he would apologize. During episodes, his pulses ran in the 120/ minute range.

These behaviors had persisted in spite of being on 300 mgs of thioridazine per day. When I saw him, I discontinued the thioridazine and placed him on the beta-blocker propranolol 90 mgs/day. On propranolol, his pulses were in the 60-70 beats per minute range and his obsessive social activities began responding to behavioral intervention. He had no rage reactions for over six months, but his pulse continued to drop, requiring a gradual reduction of propranolol to 20 mgs/day. Within two weeks of a trial discontinuation of the propranolol, he had a rage reaction with a pulse rate of 120/minute. He was put back on 60 mgs of propranolol daily with good results.

Hope for the Violently Aggressive Child

COMMENT: When I treated this patient in the early 1980s, he was a resident of an institution for developmentally disabled people. After he was given sufficient propranolol to lower his heart rate to more normal levels (below 80 beats/ minute), not only did his rage reactions disappear, but his obsessive-compulsive drives nearly vanished.

Note that this patient's heart rate spontaneously dropped so low that the propranolol had to be lowered and finally stopped. After the rages and the obsessive-compulsive symptoms returned, he was again placed on propranolol and tolerated a steady dose of 60 mgs/day for several years. I have no explanation for his change in tolerance, but such an event emphasizes the need for a regular heart rate monitor for people taking adrenaline-acting medications.

In that same institution, nearly one tenth of the population showed enough adrenaline over-reactivity to warrant treatment with propranolol. There were criticisms at that time of my use of a "heart medicine" for psychiatric purposes and for my prescribing medication for a "non-indi- cated" purpose.

One expert who came to review the case files said that patients were "toxic" on their medications. He attributed their improved behavior to placebo effect because they were being visited by an "enthusiastic psy- chiatrist" (me).

Prior to my treatment, many of these patients had been on a dose of anti- psychotics five times as high as what is considered today the maxi- mum dosage. In addition, they had been receiving injections of antipsy- chotic "as needed" when they had rage episodes. It is to be noted that within two years of initiating propranolol therapy, the nursing staff decided it was unnecessary to keep injectable medications available in every cottage.

CHAPTER 7

In 1985, I became the director of an inpatient psychiatric unit specializing in treatment of developmentally disabled and brain-injured psychiatric patients. Special protocols using beta-blocking medications were adopted. Many of the cases admitted to the unit for "aggression" were helped markedly by beta-blocking medication therapy, but these successes were tempered by the fact that nearly fifty percent of the individuals who improved during their hospital stay regressed and became violent again after discharge, sometimes within two weeks.

During the decade of the '80s, I had used beta-blockers extensively, and saw many failures as well as successes. I was able to distinguish some patients who did not stabilize because they had other psychiatric conditions such as bipolar disorder or schizophrenia. However, some patients continued to show violence and rage reactions while demonstrating no evidence of any other psychiatric disorder.

Much like other clinicians in the '80s, I could not explain or predict which individuals would respond to the beta-blocker therapy, and which would fail to respond until an unexpected breakthrough occurred with the following case.

CASE #5: DISCOVERY OF "ALPHA-ADRENERGIC RAGE REACTIONS" (LATE 1980s)

I began treating a 25-year-old developmentally disabled man with a long history of violence and psychosis. I admitted him to the hospital and placed him on propranolol, gradually raising the dose to 120 mgs/day to treat his frequent rage reactions. I replaced his antipsychotic medicine because it had a drug interaction with propranolol. He seemed to stabilize on the new combination of propranolol and haloperidol, so I discharged him.

Hope for the Violently Aggressive Child

Over the ensuing weeks, he had significantly *fewer* rage reactions than before the medication changes. However, when he did have episodes, they were different and far more severe than in the past. Before the hospitalization, his rage reactions had been fairly well controlled with staff intervention, but since his return home on the new medication regimen, he could no longer be calmed down by caregivers when he got upset. Also, he would get a different facial expression during episodes which staff described as "evil-looking" eyes, and he no longer apologized for his behavior afterwards. This patient's new type of rage behavior did not reflect anxiety and fright as it had in the past, but instead looked like the "focus/fight" crisis state of a predator (his "crazed" facial expression and focused attacking reminded one of a shark in a feeding frenzy).

I reviewed the medication changes I had made and found a scientifically reasonable theory for what had happened. I realized that there was a significant difference between the antipsychotic I had discontinued and the replacement I had prescribed. The thioridazine he had been on prior to hospitalization had a strong alpha-1 blocking effect, whereas my replacement antipsychotic (haloperidol) had no alpha-1 blocking action. In addition, his blood pres- sure during these new "predator rages" had high readings in both numbers (around 170/110), which indicated stimulation of alpha-adrenergic receptors in the blood vessels.

I then prescribed the alpha-blocking medication doxazosin—commonly known by the trade name Cardura—which had no drug interactions with his other medications. The addition of Cardura eliminated the psychotic-looking rage reactions, giving strong evidence to the idea that thioridazine's alpha- blocking effect had in the past inadvertently been preventing this patient from developing "psychotic" alpha adrenaline rage reactions, which he began having when it was discontinued.

The beta-blocker I had prescribed did reduce the number of times per week that he had beta adrenaline rage reactions. However, he had developed a new type of rage reaction based on alpha adrenaline system over-reactivity, and those rage episodes had more severe, psychotic-looking symptoms until the alpha-1 blocker was added.

COMMENT: This patient demonstrated not one type of adrenaline arousal, *but two distinct types.* The standard "fight/flight" understanding of adrenaline arousal was originally described by a Harvard scientist named Walter Cannon.[21] Cannon discovered a substance secreted into the blood from the adrenal gland during times of stress. The substance came to be known as "adrenaline." Cannon recognized that the substance prepared the body to handle crises, especially coming from environmental threats. He described the crisis arousal as the "flight/fight" reaction.

I would not have been able to figure out how to treat Case #5 successfully, however, if there had not been additional behavioral studies in the 1950s and 1960s that provided a more specific knowledge of adrenaline system activity. This research distinguished between epinephrine (beta) activity and norepinephrine (alpha) activity.

In these studies, the beta (epinephrine) arousal was identified as being related to "fear" or "security-seeking," and alpha (norepinephrine) arousal was identified as being related to "attack" or "domination."[22] In a 1966 book *The History of Psychiatry,* that research was described in the following way:

---

21. Cannon, W.B. Bodily Changes in Pain, Hunger, Fear, and Rage. New York: D. Appleton and Co., 1915 (1932 edition).

Hope for the Violently Aggressive Child

Among the experimental studies of the physiological consequences of emotional stress, those of D.H. Funkenstein and his collaborators are significant. In the laboratory they created emotional-stress situations in their experimental subjects and succeeded in establishing differences in physiological responses to anger and fear. Whereas Cannon considered the overall physiological reaction to anger and fear as being the same, Funkenstein was able to differentiate between the physiological responses to fear and anger. These studies confirmed the view of Von Euler and some other investigators that rage increases the nor-adrenaline (norepinephrine) production of the adrenal medulla, whereas anxiety mobilizes adrenaline (epineph- rine) production. The generally accepted view that endocrinological secretions are influenced by emotional stress now became enriched by a more precise knowledge of the specific nature of these psycho- endrocrinological processes.[23]

I had personally learned about the distinction between epinephrine and norepinephrine arousal states in 1957 during medical school from physiologists who were studying the dynamics of blood flow on astronaut candidates at Wright Patterson Air Force Base in Dayton, Ohio. While conducting stress experiments on the candidates, the scientist Dr. H. McChesney Goodall and his team recognized that their subjects exhibited two distinct states of adrenaline stimulation, each induced by a different type of psychological crisis experience.[24]

---

22. Funkenstein, D.H. "The Physiology of Fear and Anger" Scientific American, 192(5):74-80, May 1955

23. Alexander, Franz in The History of Psychiatry, New York:Harper and Row, 1966. Page 398.

CHAPTER 7

The first type of adrenaline state was an anxious, frightened, excessive beta state (high levels of epinephrine). In this state, the heart operated as an efficient pumping machine bringing oxygen and energy to the body, but it did not produce the blood vessel dynamics necessary to tolerate the gravity force (G-force) required for space travel. (In other words, the subjects blacked out.)

The second type of adrenaline state was a confident alpha state (high levels of norepinephrine). In this state, blood vessels constricted and mental focus allowed the astronaut candidate to tolerate the G-force. However, the heart was pumping blood into narrowed blood vessels, a situation that is not physiologically sound over time. The team concluded that extended alpha states (high-level norepinephrine output) were to be avoided unless absolutely necessary.

The investigators described one type of hyper-adrenergic state as the "prey FRIGHT/flight" state and labeled the other the "predator FIGHT/flight" state.

These labels referred to discoveries about significant distinctions between the adrenaline systems of herbivores and predators in the animal world.

Herbivores (plant-eating animals) secrete a higher percentage of epinephrine from the adrenal gland and thus have more tendencies toward beta-adrenergic arousal. Conversely, predators (meat-eating animals) such as lions are more likely to experience alpha-adrenergic arousal because their adrenal glands secrete a high level of norepinephrine. Dr. Goodall had frozen specimens sent to him from Africa of the adrenal glands of lions and antelopes to confirm this theory.[25]

---

24. Goodall McC., Meehan J.P. "Correlation of 'g' tolerance to urinary adrenaline and noradrenaline." Abstr. Proc Amer Physiol Soc Meeting. Rochester, 1956.

Hope for the Violently Aggressive Child

Dr. Goodall's team needed to be certain of their pronouncements to NASA. They even took a potential astronaut and deliberately tried to make him feel fearful that he was going to wash out of the program—and then found that he was less tolerant of high G-forces (because of the fearful, beta reaction caused by high levels of epinephrine in the blood). Later, they built the same trainee up with confidence before a test and he tolerated much higher G-force. In those trials, it was the norepinephrine level that was high.

My experience with treating Case #5 helped me realize that Goodall's work concerning fear versus dominance was a key for understanding and treating the different types of adrenergic rage reactivity.

My patient's initial rage reactions had appeared to be classic beta-adrenergic over-reactivity based in fright and anxiety, with physical symptoms of anxiety, unfocused aggression, and the ability to be calmed by strong, comforting authority figures.

The "new" rage reactivity he developed after the medication change with the "crazy eyes" and lack of remorse resembled more the characteristics of an angry, dominant predator.

The successful treatment of the patient's new rage episodes with the addition of the alpha-blocking medication Cardura confirmed to me that there were two types of adrenergic rage reactions, with distinct behavioral and physical differences, and that individuals can transition from one state to the other.

A further connection helped support the concept of the norepinephrine-based "predator" rage state. The look in the eye of a person in an

---

25. Goodall McC. "Studies of adrenaline and noradrenaline in mammalian heart and suprarenals." Acta Physiol Scand Suppl. 1951; 24(85):7-51.

alpha-adrenergic "predator" rage resembles the cold, scary eyes of a shark during a feeding frenzy. Another confirmation was made through blood pressure monitors during episodes, which demonstrated that at these times, patients did indeed have a markedly elevated reading of both numbers.

This case showed me that treatment of adrenergic rage reactions may require beta-blocking medications alone, or a combination of beta- and alpha- blocking medications, depending on the behavioral characteristics and the physical symptoms of the rage episodes themselves.

Since the "predator" rage seemed associated with vasoconstriction related to alpha-1 stimulation, *I now considered the beta-1 selective blockers preferable to the non-selective ones in most cases* (because beta-1 blockers have less of a tendency to cause vasoconstriction as a side effect). From this point, the medication metoprolol became my beta-blocker of first choice for treatment of aggression instead of propranolol.

After this discovery, I was able to treat a majority of patients with adrenergically-driven rage more effectively than I had before I differentiated between alpha and beta arousal states.

Others continued to criticize the use of a "heart medicine" for psychiatric purposes, but many patients who had not had any therapeutic benefit on other medication regimens had a significant reduction of aggression on adrenaline- acting medicines and were able to develop much more productive and stable social lives.

I saw some patients reduce or discontinue the adrenaline-acting medicines without relapsing into rage behavior. I began to recognize that the adrenaline over-reactivity in many patients was not due to a disease state but to immaturity.

Hope for the Violently Aggressive Child

Once, I had a startling thought as I looked at one of my 30-year-old patients who was functioning well and had stopped having rage episodes. I thought, "She looks so old! Has my medication regimen done that to her?" Then I realized that she had looked much younger than her age all of her life, as well as acting childishly dependent and having violent meltdowns. Treatment had helped her mature. Now she looked her age!

On the other hand, I still did have some intractable cases. Some patients with obvious symptoms of beta and alpha rage reactions did not seem to respond to a beta-1 selective beta-blocker combined with an alpha-1 blocker, and I could not explain why. These patients continued having rage episodes despite multiple medication regimens, including trials of other medicines with adrenaline-acting effects such as alpha-methyldopa, alpha-methyl-paratyrosine, and reserpine. These were used with occasional success with my "intractable" cases, but not on a predictable basis.

In 1992, I wrote a 60-page position paper titled "Dysfunctional Adrenergic States in Psychiatric Diseases: Theoretical Concepts and Clinical Correlates" which put forward my understanding of the adrenaline systems, the distinguishing characteristics of the adrenaline arousal states and their treatment. I did not consider that publicizing it would be of much benefit because too many of my patients were on medication regimens too individualized complicated for and non-specialized physician to prescribe or adjust.

CHAPTER 7

CASES #6 & #7: DISCOVERING THE ROLE OF BETA-2 RECEPTORS IN ALPHA-ADRENERGIC RAGE REACTIONS (2010):

In the summer of 2010, a newspaper article was written about the approach Dr. Cutler and I use to treat rage behavior. This article brought a number of new patients into our care.[26] The following two cases pointed to a new under- standing about the role of beta-2 receptors in rage.

CASE #6:

A 16-year-old boy with mild developmental disability had a history of several years of rage reactions. His episodes most frequently occurred when he was told to do ordinary tasks, or when his requests for parental attention were not immediately fulfilled. He was placed on the selective beta-blocker metoprolol 50 mgs twice a day to block the beta activity of the brain during the rage, and also 1 mg of the alpha-1 blocker, Cardura, because he also had symptoms of alpha-adrenergic rage behavior.

Over the next six weeks, he seemed to be having fewer severe rages, but then began having breakthrough episodes. At this point, he was placed on 1 mg of haloperidol a day because his parents said that in the past his rages had been calmed by an antipsychotic and also because the extent of his demands for parental time were somewhat irrational. Additionally, his metoprolol was raised to 150 mgs/day because his heart rate was still running high. The change in medicine caused his alpha "predator" rage behavior to become more intense.

---

26. DeBrosse, J. "Drugs slow adrenaline, change children's lives, say doctors." Dayton Daily News. 17 May 2010. (www.daytondailynews.com/news/dayton-news/drugs-slow-adrenaline-change-childrens-lives-say-doctors-710262.html)

Hope for the Violently Aggressive Child

When this teenager was switched off of metoprolol onto a fairly low dose of Bystolic (generic name nebivolol) 5 mg per day, his aggressive outbursts stopped altogether within a week.

CASE #7:

At the same time, I treated another teenage male patient who had responded initially to metoprolol and Cardura, but then reverted to having alpha-adrenergic rage episodes. He was also switched from metoprolol to Bystolic and very quickly stopped having rage episodes and showed a remark- able improvement in socialization. When we asked this teenager to describe to us the difference since being on the Bystolic, he said that in the past, when he would become enraged when asked to do something, fifty percent of the negative feelings were related to not wanting to do it, and fifty percent were feelings of resentment that someone was telling him what to do. While on the Bystolic, he explained that although being given instructions still annoyed him, he no longer had the overwhelming feelings of resentment and anger that people were trying to control him. Thus, he was more able to rationally make the decision to go ahead and obey the undesirable request.

His parents stated that within two weeks of being on Bystolic, "He made a major change. He would not yell and scream, but could reach an agreement with us. He was able to say that receiving orders from others no longer felt like they were 'taking him over' and he could just decide to obey."

COMMENT: The patients described in Cases #6 and #7 demonstrated a side effect to the best treatment option we had identified up to that time

CHAPTER 7

for severe rage reactions that included alpha "predator" episodes: the beta-blocker metoprolol combined with the alpha-1 blocker Cardura.

The side effect these patients had was a persistence of alpha-adrenergic rage reactivity in spite of the presence of the alpha-1 blocker.

Because metoprolol has some beta-2 receptor blocking activity, especially at higher doses, it seemed probable that the breakthrough alpha-adrenergic rage behavior was secondary to the vasoconstricting effect of the higher dose metoprolol. In January 2008, the new beta-1 selective blocker, nebivolol (marketed under the trade name Bystolic), had become available. Unlike the older beta-1 selective blockers, Bystolic has little beta-2 vaso-constrictive effect, and actually can produce some vasodilatation through a mechanism not related to adrenaline activity.

After the successful treatment of these two patients, I reevaluated the medication regimens of other "intractable" patients to evaluate whether they could also be having breakthrough alpha-adrenergic rage activity because of the beta-2 blockade activity of metoprolol.

All of the patients who had no major psychiatric diagnosis showed a remarkable reduction in aggression on Bystolic. I even contacted two former patients who, before they left my care, I had put on Bystolic to prevent physical side effects (e.g., asthma attacks) in order to see whether their behavior had been improved. In both cases, they were no longer considered to have behavior problems.

Hope for the Violently Aggressive Child

A THEORETICAL OR FUTURE STUDY: IS THE ALPHA-ADRENERGIC "PREDATOR" RAGE STATE A DIFFERENT KIND OF PSYCHOSIS?"

Back in the '80s when I was trying to understand and treat the "crazy-eyed" alpha-adrenergic rage reactions characterized by a psychotic facial expression, memory loss, and change in personality, I made several observations that seemed peculiar and for which I had no answers:

- I would see patients in an out-of-control beta-adrenergic fright/flight arousal state, who would seem to escalate into a "crazy-eyed," psychotic-looking alpha-adrenergic focus/fight state. It did not seem that the beta-adrenergic reactivity had gone away, but instead that it had been taken over somehow by alpha adrenaline reactivity.

- Although I found that a low dose of the alpha-1 blocker, Cardura, was effective to prevent the conversion of beta-adrenergic rage reactions into the alpha-adrenergic "crazy-eyed rage" reactions, I began to question whether the alpha and beta rage states were as distinct as I had formerly believed.

- The effectiveness of the Cardura was puzzling. Cardura is very water-soluble, and in general, water-soluble medications do not penetrate into the brain easily. How could such a low dose of a water-soluble alpha-blocker calm all the extreme brain activity that had been present during the initial beta-adrenergic rage state?

- How can beta adrenaline reactivity suddenly "turn off" and alpha adrenaline reactivity suddenly "turn on," when alpha-1 receptors of the brain and beta-1 receptors of the brain are both stimulated by the same neurotransmitter, norepinephrine?

CHAPTER 7

Before I had even formulated those questions, I had been exposed to a possible answer at a lecture in 1984, which had presented the findings that high levels of norepinephrine in the blood supply to the brain (or at least certain parts of the brain), cause a breakdown in the integrity of the blood brain barrier.[27] This prompted the supposition that the norepinephrine in the blood stream was narrowing the arteries supplying the brain and causing the changes responsible for the switch to the "predator" rage reaction I was seeing.

There is absolutely no experimental evidence that this assumption is true, but all that we have discovered about this peculiar behavior has remained consistent with this theory.

Assuming that excessive norepinephrine-induced vasoconstriction caused some change in the brain function, how do we explain the sudden change in the teenager described in case #7, who beforehand had episodes of severe rage when requested to do things which he interpreted as being "told what to do" and then suddenly became able to decide rationally to make the choice to obey and keep the peace?

---

27. Hartman B.K. "Role of norepinephrine in brain: from lab to man." Symposium 58B. Annual APA Mtg: Los Angeles, 1984.

Hartman, B.K., Swanson, L.W., Raichle, M.E., Clark, H.B., & Preskorn, S.H. "Evidence for central adrenergic regulation of cerebral vascular permeability and blood flow" in Basic and Clinical Frontiers of Catecholamine Research, Vol. I, edited by Usden, E., Kopin, I.J., and Barchas, J. New York: Pergamon, 1979. Pages 450-452.

Hartman, B.K., Swanson, L.W., Raichle, M.E., Preskorn, S.H. & Clark, H.B. "Central adrenergic regulation of cerebral microvascular permeability and blood flow; anatomic and physiologic evidence" in The Cerebral Microvasculature, edited by HM Eisenberg and RL Suddith. New York:Plenum Press, 1980. Pages 113-126.

Hartman, B.K., Swanson, L.W., Raichle, M.E., Preskorn, S.H. & Clark, H.B. (1980) "Central adrenergic regulation of cerebral microvascular permeability and blood flow; pharmacologic evidence" in The Cerebral Microvasculature, edited by Eisenberg, H.M. and Suddith, R. L. New York:Plenum Press, 1980. Pages 127-138.

Hope for the Violently Aggressive Child

A possible explanation is that his prior adrenaline reactivity was causing a psychotic-like change in his perception. If this were the case, the "psychosis" would be totally different in origin and chemical makeup from what is commonly understood as psychosis.

Typical psychosis is presumed to be related to excess dopamine, an idea fairly well validated since antipsychotic drugs seem to eliminate psychosis by lowering dopamine activity. However, the typical reference to "psychosis" involves a patient whose episodes are chronic and who has multiple abnormalities of brain function.

However, individuals who have no history of mental illness but have Parkinson's disease (a movement disorder caused by a deficiency of dopamine) can develop psychotic thinking when they receive medication to increase their dopamine levels. If the brain receives too much dopamine stimulation at once, then the brain may misinterpret what is going on and have hallucinations, which is a psychotic-like mental experience. Sometimes the Parkinson patient can distinguish that the hallucinations are not real (they may realize they are "seeing things"), but often times they cannot.

The "psychosis" of the Parkinson patient is a situation where the brain interprets a standard visual picture inaccurately, and the interpretation has more personal, emotional content consistent with the individual's personality. For example, a person who has always been suspicious of the police may see someone walking up their drive and hallucinate that the person is a policeman. Another patient traveling in a car might look out the window at a mailbox and say to the driver, "Don't hit that little girl standing by the road." Or a person might look at floor tiles and see hundreds of distinct cartoon-like faces. Such hallucinations are not frightening once

CHAPTER 7

the individual learns to interpret that unlikely experiences are hallucinations derived from one's emotional interpretation, and not act on them.

A little girl in danger of being hit by the side of the road is more emotionally important than a mailbox; a policeman coming to your house is more emotional than a friend coming over to visit; and faces have more emotional content than random lines in a floor tile. What never happens is that the Parkinson patient would see an actual little girl standing by the road and tell the driver, "Don't hit that mailbox" or see a policeman coming up the walk and say, "Here comes a UPS deliveryman."

The idea that hallucinations can be selective and temporary as seen in the "psychotic-like" thinking of the Parkinson patient may help explain the "psychotic-like" behavior seen during an uncontrolled alpha-adrenergic rage reaction. During a "predator" or "crazy-eyed" alpha-adrenergic rage episode, the brain seems to develop a "psychotic-like" perception that every person that approaches is an intruding attacker that is trying to dominate and control him or her, and an aggressive violent response is necessary. Thus, they will attack anyone coming too close to them, misinterpret friendly gestures or words as threatening, and strike out in a targeting way toward those they perceive as enemies.

Not every person in an alpha-adrenergic rage state will be so completely delusional, but it never happens that the person sees three people approaching and thinks: "Here are three friends of mine ready to help me solve the trouble I am in. (Thank goodness they are here! I need help.)"

The temporary misperception that occurs during an alpha-adrenergic rage is different from the standard dopamine psychosis in that it can develop during a beta-adrenergic rage reaction. That is, the brain cells are very stirred up because the norepinephrine nerve fibers are excessively stimulating the beta receptors. Thus, the person develops a state of beta-adrenergic agitation with increased muscular strength, body tension, and rapid heart rate. The person is "ready for action."

When the brain perceives that the crisis is of sufficient threat and attack is required, norepinephrine in the blood stream stimulates the alpha receptors to narrow the blood vessels, which compromises the blood brain barrier and changes the function of the brain cells. The brain then reaches a "psychotic- like" interpretation of environmental clues where standard external stimulation appears threatening. This is when the person begins to exhibit the characteristic behaviors of the alpha-adrenergic rage reaction and threatens to kill his grandmother, swears at the priest, says he or she hates everyone, and attacks even beloved caregivers who get in the way—and afterwards has little remorse about the event, if any memory at all.

One apparent contradiction with this concept is that a person in a "psychotic" rage state can retain enough rational control to try to manipulate others. For instance, a person in a "crazy-eyed" alpha-adrenergic rage may sense that he is not "winning" against three no-nonsense firemen holding him. His "psychotic" misperception fades to rational thinking and he may say to them, "Let me go and I will be good," but as soon as he is released, the alpha- adrenergic rage dynamics resume and he starts attacking the firemen again.

This "in and out" type of psychotic intrusion might be a function of the arterial system: the arteries can have rapid contraction or expansion according to the adrenaline content of the blood supply. When there is extreme anger or the feeling of threat, the blood vessels are squeezed down and compromise the blood brain barrier, allowing the psychotic-

CHAPTER 7

like perceptions. However, if external situations change and start causing fear or loss of dominance, the norepinephrine secretion can decrease enough that the beta-2 effect of epinephrine can keep the blood vessels open, and below the levels that cause the psychotic-like thinking. A few seconds to minutes later, the normal integrity of the cell walls making up the blood brain barrier can be re-established.

A consistent observation of individuals with alpha-adrenergic rage reactivity is that a dominant-acting figure asserting unusual authority can elicit a momentary fear reaction. If a raging individual is startled by such an authority, he or she may be jarred back into a defensive mode for a brief moment. In my experience, when a person in an alpha-adrenergic rage was headed right towards me, I would wait until he or she was almost to me and then suddenly lunge with a wild-eyed face, grab his or her arms, and yell forcefully some- thing like "You are not going to hit me, but stay away and I'll leave you alone!" Then I would push the individual backward into space—creating the distance needed for him or her to feel less threatened. The authority taking charge must be prepared to repeat several times such "startle" confrontations before the person's adrenaline system over-arousal gradually decreases to the point that normal response is possible.

This same principle exists in the wild. Even the male lion guarding its catch will startle backward if a number of hyenas suddenly lunge at him. But that startled retreat may last for only seconds before the lion's predator dominance builds up again.

Hope for the Violently Aggressive Child

CASES #8, #9, &#10: TREATMENT OF ADRENERGIC RAGE REACTIONS IN A NON-WESTERN CULTURE:

The following three cases were recounted to me by a physician working in a developing country with significant civil unrest. This physician had consulted with me by telephone over the past few years in several cases. These case studies demonstrate that immature adrenergic dysfunction is not exclusively a phenomenon of "developed" countries.

CASE #8 – EXTREME DISABILITY IN A 6-YEAR-OLD RELATED TO EXCESSIVE BETA-ADRENERGIC REACTIVITY:

A parent came to me and said, "Doctor, will you please examine my daughter? She fights all the time, she doesn't control her bowels or bladder, and she can't speak. She is six years old. Someone told me that you help children like her."

I was standing in a guesthouse of a major city of the developing country where I was working. The cleaning woman, a widow, was standing in front of me and said she went home everyday wondering which of her other children would be injured by her violent child. The younger brother was the most vulnerable target. The violent girl "KJ" had been weaned at ten months when her mother got pregnant again. Two years later, her father was beaten by the authorities and then fled for safety to a neighboring country. That is when KJ stopped eating, stopped playing, and stopped developing. Eventually, she did eat and grow physically, but she didn't speak, was not toilet trained, and went into violent fits of rage many times a day. She slept at night, but sometimes awakened screaming and anxious.

CHAPTER 7

When I saw her, she wouldn't look at me. She clung to her mother. I tried to engage her, but she was too set on her mother. After several tries, I held her wrist long enough to count the pulse: 120/minute. The rest of the exam showed a normal looking 6-year-old girl.

What made me happiest was that it seemed that she was born with a normal brain, had no lack of oxygen at birth, and had no genetic problems. I made the diagnosis of history of depression with beta-adrenergic rage and treated her with propranolol 20 mgs twice a day. I was simply copying what Dr. Ankenman had taught me about beta rage. I know it sounds impossible, like a miracle, but within four weeks that dear little girl KJ was calm, potty- trained, and speaking in full, though not complicated, sentences.

I followed her closely for three years. She continued the propranolol, started and finished a course of antidepressants for her depression and anxiety, and did better and better. Finally she went completely off the beta-blockers and was fine. Her mother sends her to school with the other children.

COMMENT BY DR. ANKENMAN: This is an amazing example of how adrenergic system dysfunction can interfere with normal maturation. Once the excessive beta-adrenergic system activity was eliminated, this highly traumatized girl was able to make significant improvements in her social development and even stop taking medication after several years. One of America's most prominent authorities on the impact of childhood trauma on the brain, Dr. Bruce D. Perry of the Child Trauma Academy in Texas, recognizes hyper-adrenergic reactivity in children with Post-traumatic Stress Disorder (PTSD), and has used heart rate monitors and adrenaline-acting medications in treatment of traumatized children.[28]

Hope for the Violently Aggressive Child

CASE #9 – RAGE REACTIVITY IN A 12-YEAR-OLD WITH "ALPHA-ADRENERGIC FATIGUE" (CHRONIC LOW BLOOD PRESSURE WITH DIZZINESS UPON STANDING):

A 12-year-old boy was referred to me by the niece of my house- helper, who had heard of my work with troubled children. The boy "MA" came with his grandmother, and we sat in a little mud-brick room that served as my office.

MA was quiet and courteous throughout the interview. He did not say very much but explained that he always had done well in school until his classes became harder. He said he had gone from being the fifth in his class to a much lower ranking. He was worried and tried to study, but late hours and trouble sleeping made him unable to concentrate. He kept going to school, but did worse and worse, worried more and more, and became more and more tired.

At that time, according to his grandmother, he also started having angry outbursts and stopped listening to others. He would become angry about the smallest things and fight with his brothers two to three times per day. When I suggested that all boys fight, she said, "Yes, but he is much worse than normal. He is more violent than any of the boys in our neighborhood. He throws things and breaks things. It is much worse than normal." I will never forget the look on that poor woman's face when she said this. It said: "You have no idea how bad this is. I hope you believe me."

MA had other problems, too. For a year he had wet the bed at night, after having complete control when he was younger. His grandmother

---

28. Perry B.D. "Incubated in Terror: Neurodevelopmental Factors in the 'Cycle of Violence'" in Children in a Violent Society. Edited by Joy Osofsky. New York: The Guilford Press. 1997. Pages 124-149.

said he just stopped waking up to go. He had migraine headaches with vomiting every two weeks. He complained of chest pain sometimes with running and complained of always having cold hands and feet. The family had taken him to a local doctor when it started. He had apparently been given imipramine at night for his bed-wetting. It had not helped him.

When I examined him, his resting pulse was 88/minute and standing it was 92/minute. His blood pressure was difficult to take, but both sitting and standing the top number was 100. I was unable to hear well enough to deter- mine the lower number. He did not have any heart murmur or other signs of serious diseases.

I made the diagnosis of alpha-adrenergic rage reactions related to "alpha- adrenergic fatigue syndrome." I treated him with clonidine 0.025 mg at night (0.1 mg ¼ tablet). I also suggested that he take a salt-containing drink like Gatorade if he became thirsty from the clonidine.

On his return visit three weeks later, MA reported that he was much better. He was waking for the bathroom at night. He had no more chest pain, was worrying less, and when he got angry, he was able to keep it under control. His grandmother was equally happy with the results and his pulse was 80/minute both sitting and standing.

Since then, I have seen him two more times. We did increase the dose of clonidine to 0.05 mg at night. When I see him, he always says he is very thankful for the medication, even though he still has to work hard to do his school work.

Hope for the Violently Aggressive Child

CASE #10—ANOTHER CASE OF RAGE REACTIVITY AND "ALPHA-ADRENERGIC FATIGUE" IN A 13-YEAR-OLD:

I met JJ when she was 13 years old. When she was only ten months old, she was found blue under the rubble after an explosion near her house. She seemed to be normal at first, but didn't learn to walk until three years of age, or talk until about five. Over the years, her mother noticed that she didn't really understand or mature like other children; she only did what she wanted and didn't listen to others.

She was fairly manageable until the family was forced to move to the city, and their living situation became very difficult. She did not sleep well, became severely fatigued, and started attacking people who got in her way. The rage her mother described was astounding—attacking and hurting people without any reason, not remembering what she had done, and not having any remorse.

However, the girl who appeared in front of me for a consultation did not at all resemble the JJ her mother was describing. She sat quietly while her mother gave her history. She appeared tired, and her mother said that she could barely walk the thirty minutes from her house to mine. They would stop and let her rest every five minutes. Her pulse rate was 100/ minute resting, and I thought she would need a beta-blocker. However, her anger symptoms were consistent with alpha-adrenergic rage. I took her standing pulse and it jumped to 120/ minute! Her hands were like ice. She had both alpha-adrenergic fatigue and alpha-adrenergic rage. I decided to work on the fatigue first and prescribed clonidine 0.025 mg at night (0.1 mg ¼ tablet) and a rehydration drink for thirst.

Within days, JJ started sleeping again, getting her energy back, and, best of all, controlling her anger reactions. When I saw her in follow-up over the next six to nine months, her mother reported that she was calm, energetic, and no longer had angry outbursts. Unfortunately, the traumatic injury that her brain had sustained as a baby still dominated her personality.

COMMENT BY THE TREATING PHYSICIAN: This patient's rage was related to an underlying state of alpha-adrenergic fatigue. This fatigue happens when a person, even during normal sleeping hours, does not "turn off" the alpha-adrenergic activity of the brain. The norepinephrine that continues to be released at night causes constriction of the blood vessels, creating low blood fluid volume. When the body stays constantly in this state, it leads to hypotension, cold hands and feet, dizziness with standing, rising pulse or falling blood pressure with standing, and the feeling of not being rested in the morning.

Alpha-adrenergic fatigue can be further divided into two categories:

1. Those who can't fall asleep or stay asleep because the alpha arousal keeps them "wired." (Many times, they didn't even sleep well as children.)
2. Those who have alpha arousal, but sleep so heavily that they cannot awaken, they "sleep like logs." Many people have some degree of alpha-adrenergic fatigue, especially during more stressful times of their life. Consider the new mother who "keeps one ear open to hear the baby." Very few cases of alpha-adrenergic fatigue seem to be accompanied by alpha-adrenergic rage.

COMMENT BY DR. ANKENMAN: These two cases demonstrate rage reactions that were secondary to physical symptoms caused by a chronic disruption of the alpha-adrenergic system. The patients did not have enough blood volume to maintain an adequate blood pressure, especially when standing. The primary cause of this low blood volume is a failure of the norepinephrine levels to decrease at night. The brain does not "relax." When norepinephrine stimulation continues through day and night, sleep is very light and interrupted, and the body's blood vessels remain narrow all the time. Consequently, the body's fluid volume stays too low, which causes weakness, poor circulation to the arms and legs (resulting in cold extremities), and especially a significant drop of blood pressure upon standing.

Although symptoms of "alpha-adrenergic fatigue" are seen throughout the world, most patients have such mild symptoms that no treatment seems neces- sary. The two children in Cases #9 and #10 developed severe symptoms because they live in both a harsh and dangerous environment. Their situation was so stressful that the excessive norepinephrine activity that caused their physical fatigue also triggered alpha-adrenergic rage reactions. Rather than prescribing medicine to target the rage reactivity, their doctor wisely treated the underlying fatigue by giving clonidine at night. The clonidine at night provided the children with a break from the excessive norepinephrine release, which helped them sleep and also improved their fluid volume by dilating the blood vessels.

CASE #11: A FINAL "CASE" FOR FUTURE STUDY: LEARNING MORE ABOUT ALPHA-ADRENERGIC ACTIVITY AND BRAIN FUNCTION:

This final "case study" does not describe an individual patient I have seen, but represents instead a case that might be described by clinicians or researchers in the future that would provide additional understanding about how alpha-adrenergic activity affects behavioral function. It would address one or more of the following questions:

- Do fat-soluble alpha-blockers have different benefits or advantages from water-soluble alpha-blockers, and if so, why?
- Is alpha-adrenergic rage reactivity in fact caused by changes in permeability of the blood brain barrier secondary to vasoconstriction?
- In what nerve centers do alpha- and beta-adrenergic nuclei govern opposite reactions for physiological functions such as control of hunger, blood pressure regulation, temperature, aggressive actions, etc.?
- What mechanisms in the brain govern the triggering of beta-adrenergic stimulation as opposed to alpha-adrenergic stimulation when both receptors are located in close proximity and both are stimulated by norepinephrine?

COMMENT: Those are a few of the unanswered questions about the "alpha-adrenergic system" and its relationship to behavioral science that need to be explored. In some cases, the basic science may have been discovered, but is not known to clinicians, including myself.

Nevertheless, discovering the effectiveness of alpha-blocking medications in controlling the psychotic-like misperceptions that are behind many individuals' violent rage episodes should make a major difference in how we approach treatment for aggression. It is hoped that in the future many other clinicians will also experience success treating previously "intractable" aggressive patients with medication therapies that act on both adrenaline systems.

Hope for the Violently Aggressive Child

The quantity of basic science and clinical investigation for behavioral symptoms related to alpha activity in the brain is, at the present time, microscopically small. The following points are relevant to the above questions:

1. Treatment of Post-traumatic Stress Disorder (PTSD) nightmares with alpha-blocking medication (fat-soluble):

I pose the question about different potential actions and benefits of fat-soluble versus water-soluble alpha-blockers based on a significant psychiatric use for adrenaline blocking agents that has not yet been mentioned. Around the year 2000, the Veterans Administration hospitals started using the alpha-1 blocker prazosin to prevent night- mares in combat veterans with PTSD.[29] It has been used by many physicians and is quite effective in relatively low doses—generally 1 to 4 mgs/ day. Prazosin is different from Cardura in being fat-soluble instead of water-soluble, and it does not stay in the body's circulation more than six hours. It was chosen for the trial because norepinephrine levels are high in PTSD patients. Since it is fat-soluble, it is presumed to work on alpha receptors in brain tissue. The authors presented that one possible effect of prazosin is on alpha-1 cells in the prefrontal cortex of the brain.

In the past, I had tried prazosin in place of Cardura for rage treatment and thought it was less effective. On the other hand, I know of one patient whose rages stopped with Cardura but whose PTSD nightmares continued until prazosin was added at night.

---

29. Raskind, M.A., et al. "Reduction of Nightmares and Other PTSD Symptoms in Combat Veterans by Prazosin: A Placebo-Controlled Study." Am J Psychiatry 160:371-373, February 2003.

CHAPTER 7

2. Norepinephrine and opposing alpha and beta nuclei in the lower brain:

Beta-adrenergic receptors are much more abundant than alpha- adrenergic receptors in the largest portion of the brain—which is the cerebral cortex. However, in the lower brain (the hypothalamus and brain stem), alpha- and beta-adrenergic receptors occur in more equal numbers. Most of these receptors are in close proximity, located in columns of cells of the lower brain that regulate body functions such as respiration, temperature control, and blood pressure. Interestingly, both the alpha and beta receptors are stimulated by norepinephrine, yet the receptors produce opposite changes in body function. For example, the norepinephrine stimulation of certain alpha receptors will cause a sensation of hunger whereas the norepinephrine stimulation of nearby beta receptors will cause the sensation of not being hungry.

Studies have shown that stimulation of certain columns of cells in the lower brain areas of animals elicit two kinds of rage behavior, one identified as "defensive" and the other as "attacking."[30] These two distinct types of rage reactions appear to be equivalent to the alpha and beta rage symptoms that humans can demonstrate.

In posing the question about how many nerve centers exist in the lower brain where alpha- and beta-adrenergic nuclei are involved with producing opposing responses, the following case provokes interesting questions:

I once was consulted by the parent of a child on no medications who developed intermittent high temperatures up to 103 for no

---

30. Wasman M, Flynn, J.P. "Directed attack elicited from hypothalamus." Archives of Neurology 1962; 27:635-644.

apparent reason. Since he also had alpha-adrenergic rage symptoms, he was treated with Cardura and started responding immediately. Within three months, the symptoms of fevers and rage vanished and did not recur after the medicine was stopped six months later. I presume the cause of the symptoms occurred somewhere in the lower brain stem, in two centers that were near each other which were responding to abnormal norepinephrine stimulation. The ability of Cardura to treat this patient's symptoms so effectively also poses the question about the potential ability of water-soluble medications to penetrate certain parts of the brain.

CHAPTER 8

When a Child Has Rage Reactions as Well as Another Diagnosis

👾👾

THE presence of illness can hinder a child from maturing. If a child has a primary diagnosis as well as adrenaline system immaturity, it is important that both be addressed in order to provide enough stability for the child to mature.

One goal of this book is to stress that not all children who have episodes of violent aggression have an underlying mental disorder. On the other hand, many children do have true mental illness, and there are certain psychiatric conditions—attention deficit hyperactivity disorder (ADHD) and autism—in which immature, adrenergically-driven rage re-activity is likely to be a complication. In such situations, the patient's rage reactivity may continue even with successful treatment of the symptoms specific to the primary diagnosis. Because an understanding of adrenergic rage reactivity is not widespread, most physicians attribute the patient's ongoing meltdowns to be related to the primary diagnosis.

Next is a brief overview of mental disorders that might also be present in children who have adrenaline system over-reactivity:

Hope for the Violently Aggressive Child

ATTENTION DEFICIT HYPERACTIVITY DISORDER (ADHD)

The most common diagnosis given to children with agitated and aggressive behavior is ADHD. Many children are given trials of stimulant medications to treat the problem. Some with true ADHD respond and gain enough control over their impulsivity that their anger reactions also normalize.

In other cases, the stimulant medicine may have no effect, or the rage behaviors may become worse. From that point forward, parents will be sure to emphasize in the child's history that the child "can't take the stimulants."

In some cases, stimulants will have a much more noticeable effect on ADHD after adrenaline system over-reactivity is stabilized. Dr. Cutler in particular has great expertise in treating ADHD in children with multiple difficulties. Since he began using medicine to stabilize the adrenaline reactivity in such patients, he has seen marked improvement in the overall function of several of his pediatric ADHD patients.

AUTISM

Parents of autistic children are often told by their clinicians that the child's violence is due to autism. Certain medications, like Abilify and Risperdal, belong to the class of medicines called "atypical antipsychotics" and they are approved by the FDA for treatment of aggression in autism. Sometimes, these medicines may improve aggressive episodes, and parents are told the remaining aggressive behavior will go away when the dose is high enough. I do not believe that autism and aggression are directly related, because some autistic children do not have aggression. I see the aggression in autistic patients most often as a symptom of their severe social immaturity.

Aggressive behavior in an autistic child should first be approached as some- thing potentially caused by adrenaline system immaturity. Autistic children already have limitations in their capacity for socialization, which increases the likelihood that their adrenaline system reactivity will be immature as well. In my experience treating autistic patients, I find that adrenaline-acting medicines are more useful for behavioral violence, and that low dose atypical antipsychotic medications can be useful to improve socialization.

GIDDY DISINHIBITION DISORDER (GDD)

Giddy Disinhibition Disorder (GDD) is a disorder of immaturity I have identified in clinical practice.[31] In childhood, there are times when children (especially in groups) get silly, laugh at everything, giggle, and are unable to be serious. During these times, they are so taken up in enjoying the funny mood that they may not worry about getting in trouble or getting hurt, as they normally would. GDD is an exaggerated and prolonged state of that giddy mood. The child seems to laugh at nearly every event, even ones that are not funny or ones that should be taken seriously.

For example, instead of eating their food, they may drop it on the floor and laugh. When told to "stop that," they do it again and laugh. The typical toddler will do this for a few months but gradually outgrows the habit. With the GDD child of any age, typical consequences and punish-

---

31. Ankenman, Ralph. "Giddy Disinhibition Disorder: A Behavior Disorder Seemingly Related to Endorphin Imbalance." Primary Psychiatry, 2002. 9(6):63-65.

ments are ineffective, and the child seems to have no emotional reaction to anything the parent does. They have no apparent sympathy for how others react to their behavior, and they show no signs of learning through consequences or punishments.

Socially, children with GDD cannot play with others well because they do not maintain boundaries: they will push, pinch, and take away toys. When others object, the GDD child laughs and seems to find the negative interactions entertaining. As they grow older, GDD children may deliberately do things that hurt people or animals and laugh while they watch the reaction. This behavior does not necessarily reflect a malicious nature. The GDD child sees such events as entertaining, similar to the mishaps shown on America's Funniest Home Videos.

Children with GDD have another unusual behavioral characteristic that helps distinguish them from normal children just being silly—a persistent lack of seeming to feel pain. They also do not avoid pain in a usual way. These children may fall down and not cry, or when they cut themselves they don't squirm and complain when the cut is being cleaned and bandaged. They may even break a bone without complaining enough that caregivers recognize the injury. Some even seek pain or injury. Extreme examples would be purpose- fully sticking their finger in the closed side of a hinged door or wetting their fingers and putting them up to an electrical plug.

The symptoms of GDD are recognized most often by caregivers who spend prolonged periods of time with the child, and see that the behaviors are persistent throughout the child's waking hours, and not just moods of silliness. They may also be frustrated by their inability to get the child to "behave." Many GDD children given a trial of stimulant medication will "go wild."

CHAPTER 8

The two areas of difficulty in the GDD child point to disruption in the body's systems of pain control. First, these children do not react to or avoid pain in the way that other children do. Second, the GDD child seems to demonstrate a lack of "social pain" in terms of not being bothered by social authority, physical restraint, or emotional consequences of disobeying authority or being disliked by peers.

The pain system of the body is modulated through chemicals called endorphins, which are similar in action to prescription pain medicines. The GDD child acts like the endorphin level in their body is too high. When a GDD child is given a medication that blocks endorphins (like naltrexone), the giddy and disinhibited behavior is dramatically and rapidly reduced. Dr. Cutler has identified and successfully treated some cases of GDD in his practice (see Postscript).

GDD children may demonstrate alpha-adrenergic rage when authority figures try to prevent them from "having their fun"—which to them might mean hitting the dog with a stick. Children who develop "crazy-eyed" rage in such cases may respond to alpha-blocking medications, but the underlying Giddy Disinhibition Disorder also must be treated with naltrexone to control the impulsive behavior.

Fortunately, GDD seems to be an immaturity disorder and rarely a permanent personality flaw. With treatment and time, most children can develop more normal social and emotional reactions to life.

DISSOCIATION

Although dissociation is not commonly talked about, it is discussed here because it can cause aggression unrelated to adrenaline activity. Dissociation is a "survival mechanism" of the brain to block certain memories or physical actions which the brain perceives as being too painful or emotionally dangerous. Dissociation is a natural function of the brain, but it is much less common in modern cultures than it was in more primitive cultures.

For example, imagine a hunter in prehistoric times in the European forests. One day he is mauled by a bear. He then might crawl under a cliff for several days. During that time of stress and suffering, his body would be healing his wounds and his brain would most likely be semi- or unconscious. If he survives, his memory might not record any of the events of those days. He might even forget completely about the bear attack, and only have dream-like memories of hearing the voice of his grandfather in the evening breeze. What would be the survival advantage of the hunter's mind blocking the memory of the traumatic event? For one thing, he is less likely to panic at the thought of going hunting again. Also, he would not live in fear of going through such a terrible ordeal again.

When dissociation has been caused by early childhood neglect or abuse, it can precipitate aggressive or violent acts. This aggression is an expression of the person's dissociated memories. Treating the adrenergic component of the behavior may lower the intensity of the rages but will not eliminate it. Such children may "for no reason" try to hit a smaller child or animal, then later be confused about why they showed aggression. Because dissociative patients may not have a fundamental trust of people, a typical care giving relationship may not be enough to overcome the problem. Many therapists do not identify dissociation readily and waste many hours trying to address the problems rationally. Dr. Cutler has found childhood dissociative scales that make identification easier.[32]

---

32. See the Child Dissociative Checklist (CDC), Version 3 by Putnam; also the Adolescent Dissociative Experiences Scale-II (A-DES) by Armstrong, Carlson, and Putnam.

CHAPTER 9

Bipolar Disorder Revisited

❧ ❧

A LTHOUGH Part I of this book covered issues of pediatric bipolar disorder, what it addressed was the confusion between children with true bipolar disorder and children who have adrenergic rage reactions without any bipolar symptoms. When true bipolar disorder exists in a patient, however, dysfunction in the adrenaline system may still be relevant in three possible ways:

PATIENTS WITH BOTH BIPOLAR DISORDER AND ADRENALINE SYSTEM DYSFUNCTION

A child with true bipolar disorder might remain immature and thus may have adrenergic rage reactions in addition to the bipolar symptoms. The behavior survey aimed at distinguishing bipolar disorder symptoms from adrenergic rage symptoms indicated that one distinction of true bipolar disorder is mood swings that occur without any relationship to environmental events. Adrenergic rage reactions related to immaturity, on the other hand, generally occur in relationship to a recent or immediate emotional event.

But suppose an individual has both? Then one would see a person become stable on adrenaline-acting medication for their rage reactions, but later when the patient has a bipolar mood swing, he or she may regress and the rage reactions may re-emerge. In such cases, caregiver reports may sound something like this: "Since being on adrenaline-acting medication, Johnny doesn't have any severe rages like he did before. But every once in a while he'll have a bad week or two with some rage episodes.

Then it goes away. There is no knowing when these times will happen." This shows the interplay between adrenaline over-reactivity and foundational mood instability. Treating one system dysfunction may temporarily help individuals be stable for a while. Until both difficulties are treated well, the person does not experience long-term stability.

The common wisdom is that when an individual is on multiple medicines and has improved behavior, the next step is to begin reducing the medications. In my experience, individuals with multiple medications and multiple diagnoses require two to five years of stability before they can tolerate a reduction of medicine. A trial to eliminate adrenaline-acting medicines frequently can be successful after several years of stability. In some cases, the mood-stabilizing medicine can also be reduced or eliminated without a return of mood swings. If symptoms return, the medications should be restarted.

THE "KINDLING" THEORY OF BIPOLAR DISORDER

Another relationship to consider between bipolar disorder and adrenaline system reactivity is the possibility that the prolonged experience of excessive rage episodes could stimulate the nervous system to move into developing a "habit" of abnormal mood cycles.

One of the theories in the literature seeking to explain why so many people with a family history of bipolar disorder do not develop the disease, is that bipolar disorder develops through a "kindling" process.

The "kindling" process has been demonstrated in laboratory animals in relationship to seizure disorder.[33] In the experiment, a signal was given to a normal portion of the animal's brain, a signal so small that there was no evidence that the brain had any reaction. However, when the signal was given repeatedly over time, the animal began reacting to the signal, and after repeated signals, the animal's brain responded with seizure activity, even though the stimulation remained very low. Eventually this sensitized area became the source for spontaneous seizure activity in the brain. This experiment demonstrates that the brain can develop abnormal function when a particular area of the brain is subjected to repeated disruption, even when each individual event is "minor."

Thus, the kindling theory of bipolar says that mood swings may start in the brain when some portion of the brain is stimulated slightly to function abnormally. If the stimulation is repeated over time the brain then can spontaneously begin demonstrating changes that cause mood instability.

During adrenergic rage reactions, the brain is highly stimulated. It is possible that when children have repeated, extreme adrenergic rage reactions, their brains may become excessively sensitized. With the idea that bipolar disorder could be "kindled" by the repetition of abnormal, excessive stimulation over time, preventing adrenaline over-reactivity with medicine could possibly help reduce the number of abnormal stimulations that are theorized to start the cycles of mood swings.

Could the disruption of the nervous system maturation and the episodes of adrenergic rage reactions be means whereby the brain is eventually stimulated to develop bipolar disorder?

---

33. Post, R.M. "Kindling and sensitization as models for affective episode recurrence, cyclicity, and tolerance phenomena." Neurosci Biobehav Rev. 2007; 31(6):858-73. Epub 2007 Apr 24.

Hope for the Violently Aggressive Child

CLONIDINE-RESPONSIVE MANIA

Another reason to believe that dysfunctional, immature adrenaline over-reactivity could contribute significantly to the course of bipolar disorder is the little-known phenomenon of clonidine-responsive mania, a form of mania that is characterized by a high heart rate and blood pressure. This type of mania is resistant to standard anti-manic drugs, but resolves rapidly when treated with adrenaline-acting medications. As mentioned earlier, a key distinguishing characteristic of bipolar mood swings is the presence of mania, and the significant factor in stabilizing bipolar disease is preventing extended manic episodes.

The idea that bipolar mania might be more quickly resolved, modified to a milder form, or even eliminated using medications other than antipsychotics or mood stabilizers has some basis in the scientific literature. During the early investigation of drug treatment of bipolar disorder in the '80s and '90s, there were some case studies published in which doctors described using the adrenergic suppressor medication, clonidine, to treat bipolar mania. These reports included cases of mania that were responsive to clonidine and had not been responsive to antipsychotics or mood stabilizers. The responsive cases often showed improvement in less than 48 hours! The studies demonstrated individual patients who had rapid and complete resolution of manic symptoms on clonidine, but only a very small percentage of manic patients showed this very positive response. Therefore, clinical trials seemed to show that clonidine was not "statistically" a better treatment for mania than placebo, and clonidine did not become an accepted mania treatment.

But trials were never done specifically on a group of manic patients with high heart rate and blood pressure, and clinical experience shows

CHAPTER 9

that manic patients with those characteristics are most likely to be clonidine-responsive. Other symptoms I have identified as possible indicators of clonidine-responsive mania include excessive talking and psychotic delusions that are less bizarre than in typical mania.

Note that the dosages of clonidine tend to be fairly high in the following case descriptions, but the effect quite rapid.

CASE STUDIES FROM THE LITERATURE: CLONIDINE-RESPONSIVE MANIA:

Cases A and B: (1984) Zubenko et al. "Clonidine in the Treatment of Mania and Mixed Bipolar Disorder" Amer J Psych (the following are excerpts from the article):[34]

A. "After 4 weeks of unsuccessful treatment on this regimen (lithium, carbamazepine, and perphenazine), a course of electroconvulsive therapy (ECT) was planned. One week before ECT, treatment with clonidine 0.2 mg twice a day was instituted because of its reported anti-manic effect, and within 72 hours Mrs. A had become asymptomatic …"

B. "… a 30-year-old man, had a history of recurrent manic episodes … he was admitted … because of pressured speech, racing thoughts, increased irritability … Clonidine treatment was initiated at 0.1 mg twice a day and the dose was increased to 0.4mg twice a day over 4 days. Mr. B improved rapidly and was euthymic within 48 hours after taking his first 0.4 mg clonidine dose."

---

34. Zubenko, George et al. "Clonidine in the Treatment of Mania and Mixed Bipolar Disorder." Amer J Psych, 141:12, Dec 1984, pages 1617-1618.

Hope for the Violently Aggressive Child

Cases C, D, and E: (1987) Maguire et al. "Clonidine: An Effective Anti- manic Agent?" British J Psych (the following are excerpts from the article):[35]

C. "A 29-year-old man … with pressure of speech, flight of ideas … and grandiose delusions … was treated … with lithium carbonate 1500mg per day for a period of 8 weeks but his mood continued to cycle. He was then, in addition, given clonidine 0.1 mg twice a day increased to 0.2 mg twice a day within 2 days. Following the increase in the dose … his Bech-Rafaelsen mania rating scale dropped to 7 (from 29)."

D. "A 60-year-old woman with a long history of manic-depressive illness… [was admitted] with a mania rating scale score of 32 … She failed to respond [to three different antipsychotic medications … she was commenced on clonidine 0.2 mg daily. She became much more settled within 48 hours and was normothymic 4 days later. Her mania rating scale dropped to 5 …"

E. "A 38-year-old male … admitted with another episode of mania … mania rating scale score was 31 … He failed to respond [to high dose IM antipsychotics] … he was commenced on clonidine 0.1 mg twice a day. He became much settled within 3 days. The dose … was increased to 0.2 mg twice a day and chlorpromazine was reduced to 100mg a day. He became normothymic within 1 week. His BR mania rating scale score dropped to 6 …"

---

35. Maguire, J., Singh, A.N., et al. "Clonidine: An Effective Anti-manic Agent?" British J Psych, 150, 1987, pages 863-864.

CHAPTER 9

Case F: Case of clonidine-responsive mania treated by Dr. Ankenman:

A 25-year-old female came to a psychologist's office for help, stating that she was not going back to the hospital. I saw her for the first time when the psychologist brought her to my office. Her recent history was six weeks of continuous manic behavior, during which she had been hospitalized twice for two weeks each time. The day after her second discharge, she presented talking obsessively and planning to go on another trip. I am including portions of the psychologist's notes (with relevant details changed to protect privacy):

> "Patient presented in a very rigid and angry state. When I first met her she was delusional, stating everyone in her family runs her life. Furthermore, she was very restless, pacing around the office and pulling things out of her purse and then putting them back in again. Her other non-verbal behaviors included frowning and very tense body position. As the session progressed she mentioned that she asked her mother to hide all the knives in the house so she wouldn't kill or hurt anyone…
>
> Between hospitalizations, she had hitched a ride to Florida with two servicemen. Her behavior became so bizarre that they took her to a mental hospital where she was admitted. This behavior included tearing up hotel rooms and the soldiers' car. She also told me she had some delusional thoughts about the soldiers—that they were generals in disguise. Eventually, the hospital contacted her mother, who drove to Florida to bring her home. The hospital told her mother they would not let her travel alone because it was too dangerous."

Hope for the Violently Aggressive Child

When I saw this patient for the first time, she was still on the medication regimen that she had received in the Florida hospital, including lithium, Navane, and Cogentin. Even though the medications seemed to have given some improvement, the patient was still frequently agitated and anxious. At my office, her blood pressure was 20-30 points higher than average and her heart rate was rapid. I gave her one tablet of guanbenz, a medicine equivalent to clonidine 0.1 mg, and I told her to take one tablet every 6 hours and return the next day. The following afternoon she reported back talking more slowly, standing still, and telling me she watched television for several hours the night before. Her blood pressure and heart rate were back to average readings. The same afternoon she visited the psychologist, who reported the following:

"The patient and her mother came to see me the next day after (Dr. Ankenman's) consultation. When I went to greet her in the waiting room, I found her joking with my other clients and she was making them laugh. She had significantly improved overnight. When we got into my office, she said she was feeling better, that the medicine did really work well and the night went smoothly with no problems. Her mother noted that she could tell by morning that the patient needed the next dose. Her overall appearance was much more relaxed than the day before. Also, she did not mention even one time any feelings that others were trying to control her life. The patient said that she really did feel better and would continue to take the medicine because it worked well for her. In my opinion, guanbenz is what made the difference for this patient. Nothing else in her life was changed except that she began to take guanbenz the day before.

CHAPTER 9

Her whole affect changed to one of a person who felt relief and a generally good mood; she changed into a much happier person almost overnight."

Though this type of mania is not common, patients who have impulsive physical over-reactivity and whose blood pressure and heart rate show excessive adrenaline arousal are extremely difficult to manage and tend to be resistant to ordinary treatment. I would suggest that anyone caring for mentally ill patients take the blood pressure and heart rate on any patient demonstrating a change in their behavior with manic-like activity. The vital sign information may indicate that the patient would respond quickly to adrenaline-acting medication.

PART IV

TALKING TO CLINICIANS

CHAPTER 10

Collecting Information

❧❧

I assume most readers of this book are caregivers, relatives, or professionals caring for a child whose aggressive episodes have not responded adequately to treatment, or whose diagnosis of bipolar disorder is in question.

If you have read this far, you probably are doing so because you recognize in the symptoms of your child potential signs of adrenaline system immaturity. If you are neither a diagnosing professional nor a treating physician, you may be wondering, "How can I find out if this is the right kind of help?"

Because you have special interest in the child's wellbeing and you are likely someone whose life is directly affected by the child's difficult behavior, you are in a position to make helpful preparations by collecting information and discussing it with the professionals whose help you seek.

In this section the goal is to help prepare you to talk with medical professionals, because the material in this book is likely to be new to them, and they are likely to be skeptical for the following reasons: a) Immature adrenaline over-reactivity and the behaviors associated with it are not well-studied in the medical community; b) This book is based on clinical expertise rather than formal research; c) Most physicians are trained to consider the medications discussed here as being outside the category of medications that treat behavioral disturbances; d) The standard tradition is that identifying a diagnosis and medication treatment is the physician's primary role, not the role of the patient or the patient's family.

Hope for the Violently Aggressive Child

If you believe that immature adrenaline over-reactivity is a potential cause of functional and social problems for a child in your care, you may want to consider the following steps:

- Collect behavioral information from others who know the child, perhaps having them complete the survey of behavioral symptoms separately.
- Collect physical information that demonstrates symptoms of adrenaline over-reactivity
- Share the behavioral and physical information you collected with a physician.
- Offer to share this book with your physician.

COLLECT BEHAVIORAL INFORMATION FROM OTHERS WHO KNOW THE CHILD

Referring to the survey of behavior symptoms, find out how others in the child's life describe the child during meltdowns. Do the answers of others match or differ from your own? Does anyone identify the child as having a "crazy-eyed" rage or having true memory loss of events during a meltdown? Are there certain caregivers who consistently have better success in calming the child? If so, what techniques or methods do those caregivers use, and do those methods support an adrenergic basis for the rage behavior, either beta or alpha?

CHAPTER 10

COLLECT PHYSICAL INFORMATION

Track heart rates

Take a heart rate with a stethoscope. It is useful for comparison to collect heart rates when the child is calm, as well as when the child is upset.

When the child is calm, you can place the stethoscope over the child's heart. One beat sounds like the two syllable word "bump-bump". Count how many beats happen in 15 seconds. Then multiply the number of beats by 4 to calculate the heart rate per minute.

When the child is upset, you probably cannot hold the stethoscope on the child for a full 15 seconds. If possible, you could try to get an approximation by putting the stethoscope on the chest for a few seconds. Try to hear the speed of three beats together, then say "bump-bump," mimicking the speed you heard verbally and counting the beats for 15 seconds. Then multiply the number of beats by 4 to calculate the heart rate per minute.

If the child is so agitated that you cannot listen for even a few seconds, take the heart rate as soon as the child is calmed enough for you to listen to a few beats, as mentioned above.

Standard heart rates per minute in a calm child under ordinary conditions usually average around 80 beats/minute. If the child runs high heart rates all the time (90 beats/min or higher) even when calm, this may indicate a state of chronic beta-adrenergic arousal (nail-biting and finger tremor are other indications of chronic beta over-reactivity). Such individuals move more quickly into aggressive behavior.

Blood pressure information

Tracking blood pressure in a child is difficult because it requires a special size cuff. Request that blood pressures be taken whenever the child is seen in a doctor's office.

Document symptoms in writing

Track the child's physical and behavioral symptoms during meltdowns. Document the days and the length of time the child has rages and describe what kinds of things the child does and how they look, particularly noting if the child gets "evil-looking" eyes, threatens anyone who confronts him, attacks others, loses memory, or if the rage was triggered by a command or an order to do something.

COLLECT RELEVANT MEDICATION HISTORY

Besides making a list of current medications the child is on, also make a list of past medications. Indicate those that were beneficial for behavior but were discontinued for some other reason. Also list medications that were discontinued because they did not help, caused side effects, or created a new problem. If the child has been on any of the following medicines, note whether they caused increased agitation: lamotrigine, Abilify, Geodon, Risperdal, Invega, Ritalin, Adderall, Prozac, Zoloft, Paxil (paroxetine).

In the list of current medications, note any that the child must take very regularly because a missed dose seems to cause breakthrough behavior problems. Also note any other unusual medication reactions, such as the child becoming hyperactive when taking a sleeping pill.

Make a list of any other diagnoses the child has been given in the past.

CHAPTER 10

WHAT ABOUT THE MEDICINE THEY ARE ALREADY ON?

In general, I add adrenaline-acting medicine to the current medication regimen, unless it seems likely that the current medications are causing problems such as activation, sedation, weight gain, etc. Even then, I do not lower any medicines too quickly, since any medication can cause a withdrawal effect if lowered too quickly.

As noted earlier, some patients have adrenergic rage reactions plus a primary diagnosis, and these cases should not be treated with adrenaline-acting medication alone.

Some physicians may believe it best to reduce or eliminate all the patient's current medications before trying an adrenaline-acting medication. If your household isn't able to tolerate a period of time with the child off medicines, tell the physician of your concerns. In such cases, I have found it effective to start one new adrenaline-acting medication then lower one of the older medications.

If a patient with rage behavior is already on clonidine or guanfacine, I will generally cut that dose down to two thirds of the original before starting an alpha- or beta-blocking medicine.

If the addition of an adrenaline-acting medication treats the patient's rage, but the patient starts to have sedation, I would reduce one of the medicines with a sedating side effect rather than reducing the adrenaline-acting medication. Adrenaline blocking medicines are rarely the principle cause of a patient's sedation, although they can lower the energy level.

CHAPTER 11

Other Treatment Considerations

❧✦

WORKING WITH THE PHYSICIAN'S DECISION

IF a doctor agrees to a trial of adrenaline-acting medicine, continue keeping records of the patient's behavioral and physical symptoms for the first three months of treatment, unless the doctor gives you alternate instructions.

After three months, you and the physician may agree less record-keeping is necessary.

If a physician is hesitant or unwilling to prescribe adrenaline-acting medication for rage behavior, it is important to respect the professional reasoning behind the decision. The purpose of this book is not to interfere with or challenge the authority of a physician who knows a patient personally, but to offer alternate therapeutic strategies for patients with intractable aggressive behaviors. On the other hand, it is appropriate to clarify when a physician is recommending against a treatment from times when a physician is unwilling to prescribe a treatment directly. Some physicians may not be comfortable starting unfamiliar medication treatment therapies, but would be willing to provide ongoing care for patients who have specialized medication prescribed by another doctor.

Until the time that adrenaline system over-reactivity is a recognized disorder, adrenaline-acting medicine can be prescribed for symptoms related to adrenaline over-reactivity under the diagnosis of "dysautonomia unspecified" (ICD-9-CM Diagnosis Code 337.9).

Hope for the Violently Aggressive Child

TO THOSE WHO DON'T WANT CHILDREN
ON ANY MEDICATIONS

There are some parents and caregivers who believe children should not take any medications related to behavior issues. In many situations this attitude serves well. If your child has mild beta adrenaline over-reactivity, it may be possible to help his or her adrenaline system mature and stabilize over time using only behavioral techniques. However, if a child has extreme beta or alpha system over reactivity, it is highly unlikely that aggressive episodes will be controlled adequately to allow age-appropriate maturation with behavioral techniques alone. Adrenaline-acting medicines can provide in many cases significant improvement in weeks so that the child can begin experiencing and developing more mature control. Some children go off the medications permanently after a year of stability.

A BOY NAMED CHARLES

It is unfortunate that there are so many individuals with rage behavior that do not have access to the potentially healing treatment of adrenaline-acting medication therapy. Our hope is that this book will put the knowledge and the leadership into the hands of the professional practitioner. I think that it is fitting to close this section with the following story, typical of a caring family trying to cope with their child's violence, trying to live a normal life, and trying to find a physician with alternatives to ineffective, standard medication regimens. I never saw this child or his parents; they consulted with me on the telephone a few times as they sought local help in their home state. Here are excerpts of the family's story written by the father of "Charles."

CHAPTER 11

Charles was diagnosed with autism at age four. He began to have primarily impulsive, "out of the blue" aggression toward others, but the episodes did not last long. As he grew older, his aggression became more intense with smashing glass containers, destroying small appliances and furniture, and kicking and punching holes in the walls. The walls of the entire house were covered in plastic and wood panels to either protect or hide the holes. He also kicked and shattered two car windshields. As he got older and bigger, the aggression became more intense and harder to deal with. By the onset of puberty, his mother could no longer be alone with him for fear of serious injury.

We had seen many physicians and taken him to many specialty clinics in an attempt to treat our son and keep him in the home. Over the years, he had been tried on a multitude of medications including Ativan, Buspar, clonidine, Depakote, Prozac, Klonopin, Lamictal, Paxil, Risperdal, secretin, Seroquel, Tegretol, Tenex, Zyprexa, and even a trial of propranolol at a low dose. Other than through sedation effect, none of the medication regimens significantly reduced the aggression or impulsive behavior.

When (Charles) was 14, his behavior began rapidly deteriorating while on Zyprexa, Xanax and Klonopin. We had done a lot of research and knew our son's heart rate was regularly about 120/ minute and we talked with physicians about a trial of propranolol at a higher dose than tried previously. Most doctors shrugged it off as "stage fright medicine." During one rage, (Charles) was taken to a hospital E.R. for admission. He was given a heavy dose of Ativan, but it still took 7 people to hold him down. After changing his antipsychotic and adding a mood stabilizing anticonvulsant, he was discharged home with slight improvement in the frequency of the rages. He was expelled from a charter school and enrolled in public school. Although self-injurious behaviors were less, aggression towards caregivers increased. Rage episodes were occurring throughout the day, sometimes only minutes apart and he was again admitted to the hospital.

This was the second time I spoke with Dr Ankenman. I was considering driving to (his clinic), but the trip would be too long for (Charles). At this time the doctor in the local hospital (the same doctor he had seen before) decided to try propranolol. The Risperdal 2 mg/day and Tegretol 800 mg/day were maintained. The doctor started him on a very low dose propranolol (30 mg/day). Unfortunately, within a few weeks, this doctor left for another posi- tion out of state. We found a doctor (about 3 hours from us) who agreed to continue increasing the dose of propranolol very slowly. I continued to monitor heart rate. Around September 2008, a new doctor took over at the hospital. He was an advocate for using propranolol for rage control and recommended increasing the dosage.

When we started seeing him, Charles was at about 100 mg/day and his heart rate was in the mid 80s. Rage behaviors had gradually improved, but they were still occurring. The dosage of propranolol was increased. By October of 2008, one year after (the first hospital- ization), we reached his current dosage of 240 mg/day. His heart rate has maintained in the low 70s.

Where we have gone in one year with Charles, in my opinion, is nothing short of a miracle. His rage behavior has almost disappeared. At our darkest place, I cried out to God and He answered. He gave us back our lives when I thought our lives were over. Charles is still Charles. He's still autistic and he still has issues, but nothing compared to where we came from. He went from ten or more severe rage episodes per day, every day (sometimes continuous), to a total of two in the last six months. Property is no longer being destroyed (I'm gradually removing the paneling from the walls) and my wife is comfortable being alone with him. And most of all he is happy. He smiles, laughs and jokes, whereas before he seemed to always be in agony.

I attribute his success to propranolol, an old, relatively inexpensive blood pressure medicine. Also, I'm sure getting to the other side of puberty helped. I'll never understand why doctors are not more prone to using this medication instead of considering it as a last resort or not at all.

Medication Addendum

✑ ✑

A SUMMARY OF ADRENALINE-ACTING
MEDICATION THERAPIES:

BETA-BLOCKERS and alpha-blockers competitively block the stimulating effects of epinephrine and norepinephrine, but individuals will vary in the amount of adrenaline they release. Some individuals may reach a therapeutic effect on low doses of an adrenaline-acting medicine, whereas others may require higher doses because their bodies release higher amounts of adrenaline.

The chief goal in treating adrenergic rage reactions is to block the beta-1 type receptor in the heart and the brain in order to prevent the body from triggering excessive adrenaline production (the source of the rage behavior).

Blocking alpha-1 receptors prevents rages from becoming "psychotic." The alpha-1 receptors in the blood vessels that supply the brain seem to be the important receptors in this action. Though it is possible that blocking alpha-1 receptors on the brain cells themselves might reduce the "psychotic" rage behavior, I have not seen proof of that in my clinical practice.

Blocking beta-2 receptors in the blood vessels appears to increase the likelihood of a breakthrough of "psychotic" rage (see Cases #6 and #7).

In most cases of "psychotic" rage, a beta-1 selective blocker plus an alpha- blocker is necessary.

MONITORING PULSE AND BLOOD PRESSURE:

When a person is first put on an adrenaline-acting medicine, it is important to monitor heart rate several times a day to make sure there are no times when the rate is too high or too low. I seek a heart rate ranging between 60 and 80 beats/minute but sometimes allow as low as 50 beats/minute if the patient's function is good. Regular blood pressures are not as easy to obtain in children, and though beta-blockers do not often cause postural hypotension, too low a blood pressure can be suspected by lack of energy. In most patients, 90/60 is the minimum allowed but some will be best stabilized at 80/50. These readings may seem very low, but the risk to the child of running a low blood pressure is not as significant as the risk of spending a childhood disturbed by uncontrollable adrenaline-driven rage reactions.

INDIVIDUAL ADJUSTMENT OF THERAPEUTIC DOSE:

Because beta-blockers are competitive inhibitors of adrenaline, the amount needed will depend upon the level of excess adrenaline that an individual's body is producing. In the story of "Charles," his pulse was high constantly before treatment with propranolol, and therapeutic benefit for both his rage and excess adrenaline reactivity was best attained at the dose of propranolol 240 mg/day. Some other individuals with rage run a normal pulse and need only a low dose of beta-blocker.

Since most psychiatrists are not familiar with the beta- and alpha-blockers, and most physicians who prescribe them do not have experience with their use as treatment for behavioral symptoms, I include here a brief listing of adrenaline-acting medications. More information is available from the pharmacy or the internet, but these sources will not have helpful information on the use for adrenergically-driven rage reactivity.

BETA-BLOCKERS

Therapeutic dosages will vary per individual; a reasonable starting dose is one of the smallest sized tablets per day for an adult, and ½ that for a child. Raise as needed to stabilize pulse rate.

LIST OF MEDICATIONS

1. Bystolic® (generic name: nebivolol): This unique beta-blocker appears to be the safest and most effective beta-blocker for treatment of adrenergic rage reactions because it blocks beta-1 receptors with minimal effect on beta-2 receptors. (The vasoconstrictive side effect of most beta-blockers makes them less desirable.) Bystolic is partially fat-soluble (able to penetrate the brain). It is not available in generic form yet, because it is new. Its cost is generally less than two dollars a day.

    Like most beta-blockers, Bystolic has a warning for patients with asthma. If a patient with asthma history needs treatment with beta-blockers, it has been my practice to place them on Bystolic, as the least likely beta-blocker to cause recurrence of breathing difficulties.

    NOTE: Bystolic does have a unique vasodilatation effect not found in other beta-blockers. There are no reports or other evidence that I am aware of concerning side effects of Bystolic related to this characteristic, but parents and physicians should be particularly conscious of this possibility, particularly since the medicine is new to the market. Dosage form: Bystolic comes in 2.5, 5, 10, and 20 mgs.

2. Toprol-XL® (generic name: metoprolol): This partially fat-soluble, beta-1 selective blocker has some beta-2 blocking action, especially at higher doses. Until Bystolic was available, I considered metoprolol the most useful beta-blocker for psychiatric purposes. It is fat-soluble enough to be absorbed into the brain but not so much to cause depressive feelings, lethargy, and vivid dreams. There is a formulation of long-acting both as a brand name called Toprol XL and a generic which allows for once-a-day dosing—and it can be crushed since the long-acting formula has extremely small pellets that retain their time-release property. The regular form requires twice-a-day dosing.

   Dosage Forms: 25, 50, and 100 mg tablets; also 25, 50, 100, and 200 mg extended release tablets.

3. Tenormin® (generic name: atenolol): This is a well-known beta-1 selective, water-soluble beta-blocker. The water solubility may make it less able to affect the receptors in the brain. It is a commonly used medication by family physicians and cardiologists for various heart conditions. It is poorly absorbed and frequently fails to cover a full 24 hours when given once a day.

   Dosage Forms: 25, 50, and 100 mg tablets.

4. Betaxolol, generic. This water-soluble, beta-1 selective beta-blocker is similar to atenolol, but can last a full 24 hours. It is more expensive. Betaxolol comes in 5 and 10 mg tablets.

5. Inderal® (generic name: propranolol). This highly fat-soluble, non- selective beta-blocker is the most well known of the beta-blockers. Some physicians use propranolol because they believe that certain conditions respond best when the beta-blocker can absorb into the brain. This

belief has not been completely validated. There is a long- acting form with a delay in release called Innopran®, but this form should NOT be substituted for propranolol long-acting.

Dosage Forms: 10, 20, 40, 60, and 80mg tablets, and propranolol ER 60, 80, 120, and 160 mgs.

6. Nadolol, generic. Nadolol is a water-soluble, non-selective beta- blocker that may be useful in lowering physical signs of anxiety. Dosage Forms: 20, 40, 80, 120, 160 mg tablets.

7. Pindolol, generic. This non-selective beta-blocker is rarely used. It is unique in being able to protect the brain from reacting to high amounts of adrenaline, yet acts as a booster when adrenaline activity is too low. It is useful in treating rage in individuals with a naturally low heart rate who cannot tolerate other beta-blockers.

Dosage Forms: 5 and 10 mg tablets.

8. Carvedilol and labetalol, generics. I do not recommend these two beta-blockers for treating adrenaline over-reactivity because the vasodilating action is through alpha-blocking effect, and the beta- blocking action is not beta-1 selective.

SIDE EFFECTS

Full side effect information is available through the pharmacy or internet. The following represents information most relevant from my experience in prescribing beta-blockers for adrenaline over-reactivity and rage:

- Side effects of non-beta-1 selective beta-blockers are generally mild, but involve any system of the body where there is a tubular channel.

Constricted blood vessels may cause frostbite, constricted bronchial tree may trigger asthma, and constricted intestines can cause diarrhea.

- Nonselective beta-blockers prevent release of sugar from the liver. In diabetics on insulin and children on stimulants for ADHD with poor appetite, there can be a danger of low blood sugar.
- Propranolol and metoprolol are the most likely beta-blockers to cause tiredness and "vivid dreams."

ALPHA-BLOCKERS

Therapeutic dosages will vary per individual; a reasonable starting dose is one of the smallest size tablets per day for an adult, and ½ that for a child. Raise as necessary for rage control. Monitor for adequate blood pressure.

LIST OF MEDICATIONS

Note that neither clonidine nor guanfacine appears in this list. These are actually alpha-2 agonists (see below).

I have used three alpha-blockers for treatment of alpha "predator" rage reactivity: two are water-soluble and one is fat-soluble.

1. Cardura® (generic name: doxazosin). This medicine is now available as a generic, but the name Cardura is well-known and the generic name is impossible to communicate to others without spelling it and having a debate about where to put the accent.

    This is a water-soluble alpha-1 blocker marketed originally for blood pressure and used also to prevent urinary retention in men with enlarged prostates. In neither use is it a first line medication. On the other hand, in my experience it has proven a majority of the time to be an excellent treatment for "psychotic" rage reactions. I find normal therapeutic dose to be ½ to 1 mg for most pediatric patients, and 1 to 2 mg /day for adults. Side effects of low blood pressure are rarely seen at these low doses.

It is important to take a sitting or lying blood pressure, then a standing blood pressure BEFORE starting Cardura, since many young adults have a drop in blood pressure upon standing. For an uncomplicated case of alpha-adrenergic rage reactivity, the patient's habit of having rages may be gone after six months of treatment, allowing a trial at a lower dose. However, it is important to seek to wait long enough before a trial lowering or discontinuation, because if the rage reactivity reoccurs, it is my experience that it will require starting the schedule at the beginning again (another 6 months). Dosage Forms: 1, 2, 4, and 8 mg tablets. A long-acting form is avail- able, but I have never had the need to use it.

2. Hytrin® (generic name: terazosin). This alpha-1 blocker can be used exactly like Cardura, but it is a powder in a capsule. It can be put into liquids if the patient cannot or will not swallow pills.
   Dosage Forms: 1, 2, 5 and 10 mgs.

3. Minipress® (generic name: prazosin). This is a shorter acting fat- soluble alpha-1 blocker. This medicine is a quite antiquated blood pressure medicine that has been shown to be effective in stop- ping Post-traumatic Stress Disorder (PTSD) nightmares. Its use is discussed above.
   Dosage Forms: 1, 2, and 5 mgs capsules.

SIDE EFFECTS

Full side effect information is available through the pharmacy or internet. The following represents information most relevant from my experience in prescribing alpha-1 blockers for adrenaline over-reactivity and rage:

- A drop in blood pressure upon standing is the most common side effect of alpha-1 blockers. At the low doses suggested for treatment of adrenergically-driven rage, this side effect is not common.
- Monitor blood pressure twice a week after the dosage is stabilized. Monitor more frequently if the dose is being adjusted.
- Some individuals may have urinary leakage with higher dose alpha-blocking medication.

ALPHA-2 AGONISTS

Alpha-2 agonists stimulate the alpha-2 receptors, which regulate the outflow of norepinephrine from the neurons that produce it. I do not use alpha-2 agonists to treat adrenergically-driven rage reactions, because they do not block excessive norepinephrine release, they only slow the release. Alpha-2 agonists are NOT alpha-blockers, nor are their effects exclusively on alpha receptors.

When I first recognized alpha-adrenergic rage, I tried to treat it using alpha-2 agonists and found that in most cases these medications were inadequate to stop severe rages from developing. When adrenaline over-reactivity is out of control (as occurs during crisis adrenaline reactivity) the alpha-2 regulator mechanism is ineffective against the flood of norepinephrine.

I do use alpha-2 agonists extensively for the less intense norepinephrine over-reactivity of the brain that is seen in ADHD, "stress-related" insomnia, and in some cases of mania (which is discussed specifically on page 109). They also can be useful to treat symptoms in the body caused by excessive alpha reactivity (like spastic bowel function and abnormal blood pressure).

LIST OF MEDICATIONS

1. Clonidine, generic. This medicine is only available as a generic. This alpha-2 agonist comes in tablets. It can be broken easily into halves or quarters. It is tasteless and can be absorbed under the tongue. Therapeutic doses generally range from 0.025 mg to 0.2 mg/dose and the effect lasts 4-6 hours.

     Dosage Forms: 0.1, 0.2, and 0.3 mgs.

     A long-acting form of clonidine lasting 8-12 hours has been available from some compounding pharmacists. Recently two different companies have placed long-acting clonidine on the market.

2. Kapvay® twice a day for ADHD. Dosage Forms: 0.1 and 0.2 mgs. Nexiclon XR® given once a day for hypertension.

     Dosage Forms: 0.17 mg, 0.26 mg, and liquid 0.09 mg/ml.

3. Guanfacine, generic. There is a long-acting preparation called Intuniv (the trade name) indicated for ADHD. Guanfacine is marketed for therapeutic calming effect in ADHD patients. It is longer-acting and less sedating than clonidine, but it is also less effective in my experience.

Postscript by Dr. Edward Cutler

❦

MY first contact with Dr. Ankenman occurred by chance. At the time, I had a 12-year-old patient with autism, who could barely communicate and had spoken only one word, "Stop!" She was becoming too violent for my office and waiting room. She broke a window, and I was afraid she would hurt younger patients. I suggested that she see a psychiatrist more experienced in handling aggression and violence. Her mother found Dr. Ankenman, who practiced in a hospital in the next county. He was the only one willing to take care of her in his office.

After a few weeks, I received a report about her progress. She was on a long list of drugs in doses that seemed to me to be too small to be helpful. I thought, "What kind of quack uses so many different drugs at such low, ineffective doses?"

A month later, the mother brought her daughter into my waiting room, which was filled with patients. I expected a disaster but was pleasantly surprised. The girl was neither violent nor aggressive and even spoke a little to me. That was the moment I decided to learn what I could from her psychiatrist, and I am still learning.

A few years later, my 90-year-old father had become too agitated and disruptive to remain at home. My mother wanted to place him in a nursing home; so I drove him from New York to Columbus, Ohio, and had him hospitalized for testing and treatment. Nobody in Columbus had anything to offer to help my father. I described his symptoms to Dr. Ankenman who said, "Try Delsym"—which is pure dextromethorphan, the same ordinary cough medicine I gave to my pediatric patients. He told me to start with one teaspoon twice a day. I followed this advice but remained skeptical—until my father improved and was able to return home to my mother, where he had another good year.

I learned from Dr. Ankenman that dextromethorphan behaves differently in some elderly because it is metabolized more slowly and then has a strong effect on the glutamine pathways of the brain. I also learned to use certain drugs for off-label indications, and that often two drugs in low doses can have more efficacy and fewer side effects than a high dose of one medication alone—even for an indicated use.

When I started using very low doses of atypical antipsychotics to promote socialization in children with autistic-like symptoms, I found them effective. However, if other pediatricians and psychiatrists saw my patients, they usually increased the doses presumably to treat the child's violence or mood swings. This often decreased their socialization and generally made them too "dull"— though sometimes the higher dose made them overactive. Dr. Ankenman's approach of using adrenaline-blocking medications to treat violence was more effective and allowed for low doses of atypical antipsychotics, which were effective in increasing social activity.

It took me a long time to accept Dr. Ankenman's theory about adrenergic blockers. At first I thought that he was "messing around" in an area where psychiatrists had no business. I had used propranolol to treat stage fright. I had also tried it in aggressive diabetics, who rebelled by refusing to take insulin. I had had minimal success. In a few of the diabetic patients, the beta-blocker masked the symptoms of hypoglycemia, causing them to act aggressive. In the rest, there was mostly a transient decrease in rage and aggression followed by a worsening of all symptoms.

POSTSCRIPT BY DR. EDWARD CUTLER

It was not until I put my first patient on an alpha-blocker as well as a beta-blocker that I became a believer. Propranolol and metoprolol by them- selves often worked only until alpha-adrenergic breakthrough rage occurred. When parents and their physicians saw this increase in the severity of rage in their children treated with beta-blockers, they stopped them—and also stopped thinking about adrenergic blockers. When I saw that the addition of alpha-blockers such as doxazosin prevented psychotic rage, I was willing to try adrenergic blockers as the first line medications to treat aggression.

Dr. Ankenman's understanding of beta- versus alpha-adrenergic rage began to change the lives of my patients. The mother of a sixteen-year-old boy was ready to canonize Dr. Ankenman after her son's behavior improved. That patient had seen many psychiatrists, pediatricians, and psychologists, all of whom diagnosed traditional conditions such as ADHD, mood disorders, and unsocialized aggression. The boy had responded somewhat to stimulants, and risperidone (trade name Risperdal), but these only minimally modulated his aggression. He punched holes in walls and exploded when his mother or teachers threatened his security. He bit his nails and picked at his skin. Sometimes he hurt his mother and immediately felt remorse. These are signs of beta adrenaline over-activity and indicate the need for treatment with a beta-blocker. Metoprolol changed his life. After a month of metoprolol, 50 mg every 12 hours, his mother stopped giving him Risperdal, which he no longer needed. For the first time rage and aggression did not dominate his life.

After a year or so, I had accumulated about fifty pediatric patients who had responded to alpha- and beta-blockers. Some of my colleagues attributed the decrease in rage and unsocialized aggression to a placebo effect.

Hope for the Violently Aggressive Child

I asked them: "For years, I have been using medicines such as stimulants, atypical and typical antipsychotics but they failed to help. Why did those medicines not have the same placebo effect?"

And when I asked parents what they would do if I stopped adrenergic blockers, they gave replies such as these: "I would break into the pharmacy and steal them" and "I would find another doctor who would give them."

An even more astounding example of the "healing powers" of the use of adrenaline blocking medicines to bring about maturity is that of a fifteen- year-old girl named Kayla. I have known Kayla since she was a toddler. She presented with all the inattentive, impulsive, and hyperactive symptoms of ADHD. She also had days and even weeks of depression followed by spells of uncontrollable hyperactivity. Her father, paternal grandfather, two paternal aunts, and one paternal uncle had been diagnosed with and treated for bipolar mood disorders, and they all improved with medication. She had frequent migraine headaches, as did her mother. She had insomnia and asthma as well.

She began having violent outbursts at age four, and they got worse and worse as she got older. She would kick, bite, and hit her mother. One time her mother tried to hold her down and Kayla called the police. In the fourth grade, she hit a boy who had taken her snack and broke his nose and ribs, and fractured his jaw. She became aggressive whenever challenged by authority. She said she didn't like "direct commands," which she said gave others control over her and made her feel "like a slave."

Stimulant therapy controlled most of her symptoms of ADHD, but not her aggressive behavior. Topamax 25 mg at bedtime prevented migraine headaches. She had failed to respond to standard mood-stabilizing and anti- psychotic medications, but when placed on metoprolol and

Cardura she became "like a brand new kid." Her teachers called home to state that she was much calmer now. After treatment with adrenaline blockers, she herself says, "I don't want to fight anymore and now more people want to be around me." Her mother trusts her to care for her younger sister, and Kayla enjoys being with her. Recently, she has begun to talk about going to college. In the past, many people thought that Kayla would either be in jail or dead by the time she was twenty.

Another group of children with severe behavioral disturbance based in immaturity which I have identified with Dr. Ankenman's help are those with Giddy Disinhibition Disorder. Though he published an article on this in 2002, other doctors have not identified that they are seeing such patients in their practices. This is a relatively infrequent disorder, and these children are often misdiagnosed with ADHD and are on stimulants. They frequently laugh inappropriately such as when someone gets hurt and may find everything funny. They are often insensitive to pain. Sometimes their mothers used drugs such as crack cocaine during their pregnancies. An imbalance of endorphins may cause this disorder. After giving naltrexone treatment to one chronically disruptive child and noting the instant benefits, I became much more sensitive to the cluster of symptoms these "giddy" children exhibit.

The first time I described Giddy Disinhibition Disorder to another physician, he insisted it did not exist and was a figment of Dr. Ankenman's imagination. I told him to tell that to parents whose child's life was changed by giving one tablet of naltrexone at bedtime. The following is a letter I received from the parent of two children I treated for ADHD and Giddy Disinhibition:

Hope for the Violently Aggressive Child

Dear Dr. Cutler,

I wanted to write you this letter to tell you thank you for helping me and my family by taking the time to listen to me about my childrens' problems. They have been on medications most of their lives but nothing had worked for them until I had brought them in to you. I had come close to giving up and basically it looked as they would end up behind bars. Close to five years ago my daughter _____ had three assault charges; all she wanted to do was fight and laugh.

Everything to (her) was funny. When I tried to explain to her she was killing me and was going to end up in jail she would laugh; she would hit me and her siblings and laugh and make fun of us when we cried. As for (my son), he would catch trash cans on fire and laugh when the fire department came. He would jump out of the car while I was driving down the road. He would fight and steal and run from me and call me names and would laugh when I cried. As for school, (both) were kicked out.

As for you Dr. Cutler they both take Vyvanse and naltrexone and they are like new children. (My daughter) is 18 and has a baby 6 months old and is a wonderful mother and we get along great, and as for (my son), he is 15 and goes to school and has his future planned to be a underwater diver for the police dept. He doesn't play with fire or steal anymore and is caring and is a very good uncle.

Thank you so much Dr. for being so understanding and finding the correct medication to make them be a productive citizen and wonderful children. You gave us all a chance at life again.

POSTSCRIPT BY DR. EDWARD CUTLER

For many years, I have treated hundreds of children. In the early days, I saw many patients on Mellaril and Thorazine as well as stimulants. Most physicians gave sub-therapeutic doses of stimulants that did little except decrease their appetite and give other side effects. They did not give them on weekends and holidays and during vacations and usually stopped them early in adolescence. I did get better results by using higher doses of stimulants and insisting the medicines be continued into adulthood. But many of those early patients I cared for never stopped having episodes of irrational aggression. Several are now in prison and some are dead.

In my opinion, the advantage of adrenergic blockers and naltrexone is that they treat immaturities and often are no longer needed after the patient matures. Even though more research is needed, I don't think we should deprive children with alpha- and beta-adrenergic rage or giddy disinhibition the benefits of treatment.

Excerpted Transcript Telephone Conversation Between Kayla and Dr. Ankenman on June 29, 2011

⤳⤶

Today I had the following conversation over the phone with Kayla, a 14-year-old patient of Dr. Cutler's.

Dr. A: Hello, Kayla, this is Dr. Ankenman. Do you remember talking to me at Dr. Cutler's office on his telephone?

Kayla: Yes, I remember.

Dr. A: Your mother said that you would be willing to talk about your anger with me for my book.

Kayla: Yes, I am.

Dr A: Do you want us to use your name, Kayla?

Kayla: Yes.

Dr A: Do you want a picture in the book? K: Yes.

Dr A: Do you have a picture? K: I have lots of them.

Dr A: Okay. People don't understand individuals when they have this special anger. Others will say to them, when you were angry and you did something or other, and the person who was angry says "No I didn't. The parent or teacher will say, "You are just trying to cover up." Did that ever happen to you?

K: A lot.

Dr A: What did it make you think?

K; I thought they were crazy. I didn't do that.

Dr A: Why did you think they always kept saying it? K: I didn't know.

Dr A: Did you say to yourself I couldn't have done that?

K: Sometimes. Sometimes I thought I could have done it depending upon what it was, but sometimes I didn't think I did it.

Dr A: Can you give me example of something they said you did that you would never believe that you would do?

K: They said I broke a kid's face because he stole my animal cracker.

Dr A: And you don't think you would have done that?

K: No.

Dr A: But you realize now that you did?

K: Yes. And I threw an easel at my teacher. I threw a lot of stuff at my teacher. They said that I cussed my teacher out and I don't remember doing that either. I was only like 4 years old.

Dr A: So you didn't normally cuss? K: No I didn't.

Dr A: So did you ever think, "There is something wrong with me?"

K: Occasionally, but you know, but mostly I would think these people are crazy. I didn't do that.

Dr A: When did you first realize you had this blackout type anger?

K: When I was in the 3rd grade my friends told me what I was doing and that I was getting into fights.

Dr A: One of the feelings of growing up is to take control. How do you feel about yourself? Did it make you feel inferior because you couldn't control yourself?

K: It made me feel like I was dangerous. Dr A: So you couldn't trust yourself?

K: I didn't have control of myself, and I knew that I was strong.

TRANSCRIPT TELEPHONE CONVERSATION

Dr A: Did you ever not make friends because you didn't want to do something to them?

K: I was very unsocial in school. I didn't have any friends in elementary school.

Dr A: So what did you do?

K: I stayed in the corner at recess in my jacket cause it was cold in the school when it was winter, and when it wasn't cold outside I still stayed in the corner by myself.

Dr A: Did anyone ever call you autistic? K: No.

Dr A: Had other doctors looked at you? K: Yes.

Dr A: Did they put you on medicine?

K: They tried to. All they wanted to do was up the medicines I was already on and like zombify me.

Dr A: What medicines were those? K: Like Seroquel.

Dr A: One of the things people have told me, that got over this, is that when they get an order from somebody, it sounds like someone is trying to take you over—be in control—treat you like a puppet.

K: I don't like it when people tell me what to do. It is the one thing that sets me off. Like it makes me so mad when someone tries to tell me what to do.

Dr A: You still have trouble with that?

K: I'm doin' better with it now. Used to be that I would just want to punch them in the face.

Dr A: Why?

K: I don't know why. I didn't like them telling me what to do. It felt like they had control over me.

Dr A: One kid said to me "It used to be when my parents would tell me to do something 50% would be cause I was lazy and didn't want to do it, and the other 50% I wouldn't want to do it because I didn't want anybody ruling me. Now I can handle the part about not wanting to, and go ahead and do it."

K: That's how I am. I'm lazy too.

Dr A: It is sort of like somebody saying to you we are going to put you on a boat and take you somewhere and make you a slave. "Get on the boat!" Are you going to want to step on the boat?

K: No.

Dr A: Is that the way you feel? K: Yes.

Dr A: You can feel that way even if you're not angry. But do you get instantly angry?

K: I get instantly angry. It makes me like, instant mad.

Dr A: So how is it now? Is there any difference now on the medicine?

K: There's a big difference now. Like now I can do stuff that mom tells me what to do. I still kinda don't like her telling me what to do, but it doesn't make me mad.

Dr A: Why do you do it?

K: I don't know. I think it's the medicine. The medicine helps me a lot.

Dr A: The reason you do it is you want to be social and get along with people. It's a natural feeling to want that. Do you agree?

K: Yes.

Dr A: Before you had that feeling but you couldn't give yourself up because you wanted to be independent and run your own life?

K: Yep.

Dr A: So now you can choose to do something for somebody, but it's not easy?

K: But I can if I want to.

Dr A: How old are you now? K: Fourteen.

Dr A: What year of school are you in? K: I'm in 9th grade.

Dr A: Have you always been a good student? K: I used to be but recently I haven't been.

Dr A: I heard that you were talking about going to college. K: I want to go to college.

Dr A: What do you think you'll be like when you're 25?

K: I'm going to be awesome. I'm going to have lots of money. I want to be like famous for something. I don't care for what I just want to be famous for something.

Dr A: You always felt that way?

K: Yeah. Not really. No I didn't really want to be famous when I was little. Dr A: How has being on this medicine helped you?

K: It tames me—like I have friends now. I have people I can call. I actually have people in my phone and people actually call and text me first. And I actually just came back from hanging out with one of my friends. And I can talk to my family and hang out with my family without problems all the time and end up fighting with them all. I've gotten out of trouble with the police because the cops don't have to come for me a lot because I fight with my mom anymore.

Dr A: Do you know any of the teachers that knew you before you got on the medicine?

K: Yeah.

Dr A: What do they say now?

K: They say they wish they had me when I was like that. Mr. _____, one of my teachers who had me when I was in 6th grade and he was like "I tried all year with Kayla. I wish she had been like that when I had her."

Dr. A: People were trying?

K: Yes, they knew I was a good student. They didn't know how to fix my problems.

Dr A: Did you ever meet anyone who just said you were a lousy nasty person and gave up on you?

K: Not really. All my teachers have always tried on me.

Dr A: That's because they saw the real you underneath. How long do you think you will have to be on the medicine?

K: I don't know.

Dr A: If you had to take it for life would you take it? K: Yes.

Dr A: You probably won't have to be. What do you think was wrong with you?

K: It was there was like a little mean person in my brain telling me what to do; and it wasn't me it was just there.

Dr A: Does that mean you're a crazy person? K: Yes I'm crazy.

Dr A: Not really. That little thing in there is what we call instinct. You were born with it. Everybody is born with it. Most people get rid of it when they are cuddly little babies and they give up being an isolated individual because it is more fun to be with people. Some people don't give it up and it becomes sort of a second personality. But all it is—is being not in control, and you should be able to learn control; then you could go off the medicine. There's no hurry. The medicine is not that hard to take; is it? Does the medicine bother you?

TRANSCRIPT TELEPHONE CONVERSATION

K: Not really. I don't even notice it when I take it.

Dr A: What would you say to someone who had your anger problem and didn't want to take the medicine for it?

K: I would tell them they were crazy—and they would want to fight me over it.

Dr A: It's well worth taking then?

K: Yes it is.

Works Cited

Ahlquist, R. (1948). A study of adrenotropic receptors. *Am J Physiol, 153* (3), 586-600.

Alexander, F. (1966). *The History of Psychiatry.* New York: Harper and Row. Ankenman, R. (2002). Giddy Disinhibition Disorder: A Behavior Disorder Seemingly Related to Endorphin Imbalance. *Primary Psychiatry,* 9 (6), 63-65.

Cannon, W. (1915 (1932 edition)). *Bodily Changes in Pain, Hunger, Fear, and Rage.* New York: D. Appleton and Co.

DeBrosse, J. (2010, May 17). Drugs slow adrenaline, change children's lives, say doctors. *Dayton Daily News* www.daytondailynews.com/news/dayton-news/drugs-slow-adrenaline-change-childrens-lives-say-doctors-710262.html.

Elliott, F. (1977). Propranolol for the control of belligerent behavior following acute brain damage. *Ann Neurol, 1,* 489-491.

Freedman, A.M., et al. (1976). *Modern Synopsis of Psychiatry: 2nd edition.* Baltimore: Williams & Wilkins Co.

Funkenstein, D. (1955). The Physiology of Fear and Anger. *Scientific American,* 192 (5), 74-80.

Goodall, McC., et al. (1956). Correlation of 'g' tolerance to urinary adrenaline and noradrenaline. *Proc Amer Physiol Soc Meeting.* Rochester.

Goodall, McC. (1951). Studies of adrenaline and noradrenaline in mamma- lian heart and suprarenals. *Acta Physiol Scand Supp, 24* (85), 7-51.

Hartman, B.K. (1984). Role of norepinephrine in brain: from lab to man (Symposium 58B). *Annual APA Mtg.* Los Angeles.

Hartman, B.K. et al. (1980). Central adrenergic regulation of cerebral microvascular permeability and blood flow; anatomic and physi- ologic evidence". In *The Cerebral Microvasculature* (pp. 113-126). New York: Plenum Press.

Hartman, B.K. et al. (1979). Evidence for central adrenergic regulation of cerebral vascular permeability and blood flow. *In Basic and Clini- cal Frontiers of Catecholamine Research, Vol. I* (pp. 450-452). New York: Pergamon.

Jefferson, J. (1974). Beta-adrenergic receptor blocking drugs in psychia- try. *Arch Gen Psychiatry, 31* (5), 681-91.

Kaplan, S. (2011). *Your Child Does Not Have Bipolar Disorder: How Bad Science and Good Public Relations Created the Diagnosis.* Santa Barbara: Praeger.

Kraepelin, E. (translated into English 1921). *Manic-Depressive Insanity and Paranoia.* www.onread.com/book/ Manic-Depressive-Insanity-And-Paranoia-82583.

Maguire, J. et al. (1987). Clonidine: An Effective Anti-manic Agent? *British J Psych*, 863-864.

WORKS CITED

Moreno, C., et al. (2007). National trends in the outpatient diagnosis and treatment of bipolar disorder in youth. *Arch Gen Psychiatry, 64* (9), 1032-1039.

Parens, E., et al. (2010). Controversies concerning the diagnosis and treatment of bipolar disorder in children. *Child Adolesc Psychiatry Ment Health, 4* (9).

Perry, B. (1997). Incubated in Terror: Neurodevelopmental Factors in the 'Cycle of Violence'. In J. Osofsky (Ed.), *Children in a Violent Society* (pp. 124-149). New York: The Guilford Press.

Pitts, F. (1985). Beta-blockers and their utility (Symposium 9D). *APA Annual Mtg.* New York.

Post, R.M., et al. (2008). Incidence of childhood-onset bipolar illness in the USA and Europe. *Br J Psychiatry, 192* (2), 150-1.

Post, R.M., et al. (1996). A speculative model of affective illness cyclicity based on patterns of drug tolerance observed in amygdala-kindled seizures. *Mol Neurobiol, 13* (1), 33-60.

Post, R.M., (2007). Kindling and sensitization as models for affective episode recurrence, cyclicity, and tolerance phenomena. *Neurosci Biobehav Rev, 31* (6), 858-73.

Preskorn, S. et al. (1980). Central adrenergic regulation of cerebral microvascular permeability and blood flow; pharmacologic evidence. In *The Cerebral Microvasculature* (pp. 127-138). New York: Plenum Press.

Raskind, M. (2003). Reduction of Nightmares and Other PTSD Symptoms in Combat Veterans by Prazosin: A Placebo-Controlled Study. *Am J Psychiatry, 160*, 371-373.

Sorgi P.J., et al. (1986). Beta-adrenergic blockers for the control of aggressive behaviors in patients with chronic schizophrenia. *Am J Psychiatry, 143* (6), 775-6.

Suzman, M. (1971). The use of β-adrenergic blockade with propranolol in anxiety symptoms. *Postgrad Med J, 47*, 102-107.

Wasman, M., Flynn, J. (1962). Directed attack elicited from hypothalamus. *Archives of Neurology, 27*, 635-644.

Williams, D.T., et al. (1982). The effect of propranolol on uncontrolled rage outbursts in children and adolescents with organic brain dysfunction. *J Am Acad Child Psych, 21*, 120-135.

Yudofsky, S. et al. (1981). Propranolol in the treatment of rage and violent behavior in patients with chronic brain syndromes. *Am J Psych, 138*, 218-220.

Zubenko, G. et al. (1984). Clonidine in the Treatment of Mania and Mixed Bipolar Disorder. *Amer J Psych, 141* (12), 1617-1618.

Index

A

ADHD. *See* Attention deficit hyperactivity disorder (ADHD)
Adrenaline-acting medications, 26, 36
Adrenaline-based reactivity, iii, 26
    alpha, 38–39, 40–41
    beta, 37–38
    with bipolar disorder, 113–114
    epinephrine, 52–53
    immaturity, 85
    norepinephrine, 52
    two types of adrenaline arousal, 48*f*
    and violence, 44–45
Adrenaline crisis
    alpha adrenaline activation, 64–65
    beta adrenaline activation, 63–64
    physiology, 65–66
Adrenaline receptors
    alpha, 53
    beta, 53
    in brain, 56
Adrenal systems
    arousal, 36
    and behavior, iii–iv

crisis reflexes, 26

cruise ship model, 57–61

epinephrine, 51

immature, 25

norepinephrine, 51

stress, iii–iv

survival, 39–40

Aggressive behavior, ii

and adrenal reactivity, 45

and adrenal systems, iv

immaturity, iv

terminology, viii

treatment of excess adrenaline reactivity, 26

Alpha adrenal system, 38–39, 40–41

versus beta adrenal system, 54–55

and bipolar diagnosis, 39

of herbivores, 83–84

mechanism, 55

and norepinephrine, 52

of predators, 83–84

Alpha-adrenergic fatigue, 98–99, 100–102

Alpha adrenergic reactions and rage

with alpha-adrenergic fatigue, 98–99, 100–102

with attention deficit hyperactivity disorder (ADHD), 108

with autism, 108–109

and beta-2 receptors, 87–89

and blood-brain barrier, 103

definition, 46

discovery of, 79–86

with dissociation, 111–112

with giddy disinhibition disorder (GDD), 109–111

in non-Western cultures, 96–102

physical symptoms, 64–65

as psychosis, 90–95

signs, 47

startle confrontations, 95

Alpha-blockers

Cardura® (doxazosin), 142–143

Hytrin® (terazosin), 143

Minipress® (prazosin), 143

side effects, 144

Alpha-blocking medications

Post-traumatic Stress Disorder, 104

psychotic-like misperceptions, 103

Alpha-2 agonists

clonidine, 145

guanfacinem, 145

Kapvay®, 145

usage, 144–145

Anxiety

beta-blocking medications, 71–74

definition, 72–73

epinephrine, 73

serotonin antidepressant medications, 73–74

Arterial intrusion, 94–95

Atenolol. *See* Tenormin® (atenolol)

Attention deficit hyperactivity disorder (ADHD), 23, 108, 150–151
Autism, 108–109, 133–135

B

Behavior management considerations, violent aggression, 49–50
Behavior survey, xi–xiv
Berserkers, 40
Beta adrenal system, 37–38
    versus alpha adrenal system, 54–55
    and epinephrine, 52
    and heart, 55–56
    mechanism, 54–55
Beta-adrenergic reactions
    and brain injury, 69–71
    definition, 45
    epinephrine, 53
    physical symptoms, 63–64
    signs, 45–46
Beta-blockers
    betaxolol, 140
    Bystolic ® (nebivolol), 139
    carvedilol, 141
    Inderal® (propranolol), 140–141
    labetalol, 141
    nadolol, 141
    pindolol, 141
    side effects, 141–142

INDEX

Tenormin® (atenolol), 140

Toprol-XL® (metoprolol), 140

Beta-blocking medications

and anxiety, 71–74

and heart rate, 75

and hyperactivity, 74–77

and rage, 77–79

Beta-2 receptors in alpha-adrenergic rage reactions, 87–89

Betaxolol, 140

Bipolar disorder and diagnosis

absence of mania, 25

with adrenal system dysfunction, 113–114

and alpha adrenal response, 39

in America versus Europe, 21

characteristics of, 28–29

clonidine-responsive mania, 116–121

concerns about, 20

controversy about, iii, 19–20, 22

as diagnosis du jour, 23

versus immature adrenaline system, 25

increase in diagnosis, 19–20, 21

kindling theory, 114–115

as manic depression, 27–28

manic episodes, 30–31

misapplication of for behavior disorders, 23

misdiagnosis of, viii

mood swings, 27

option of convenience, 20

psychotic break, 29–30
Blood brain barrier, 91
Blood pressure medicines, i–ii
Brain,
    and adrenal receptors, 56
    beta-adrenergic rage, 69–71
Bystolic® (nebivolol), 88, 139

C

Cardura® (doxazosin), 88, 90, 106, 142–143
Carvedilol, 141
Clonidine, 99, 100, 145
Clonidine-responsive mania, 116–121
"Controversies concerning the diagnosis and treatment of bipolar
disorder in children" (*Child & Adolescent Psychiatry and Mental Health*,
March 2010), 22
Cruise ship model, adrenal systems, 57–61
Cutler, Dr. Edward, 147–153

D

Dextromethorphan, 148
Diagnosis
    and adulthood, implications for, 25
    epidemics, 23–24
    expectations of, 24
Dissociation, 111–112

Doxazosin, 80–81. *See also* Cardura® (doxazosin)

Dysautonomia unspecified, 131

E

Epinephrine
 and anxiety, 73
 and beta receptors, 53
 definition, 52
 distinction from norepinephrine arousal state, 81–83

F

Fight/flight reaction, 81–82

G

GDD. *See* Giddy disinhibition disorder (GDD)

Giddy disinhibition disorder (GDD), 109–111, 151–152

Guanfacinem, 145

H

Hallucinations, 92–93

Heart, and adrenal receptors, 55–56

Hyperactivity, and beta blocking medications, 74–77

Hytrin® (terazosin), 143

I

Immaturity, iv, 25, 85
Inderal® (propranolol), 140–141
Information collection
    behavioral, 126
    physical, 127–128
    relevant medication history, 128–129
Instincts
    and control, loss of, 160
    definition, 43
    purposes, 43
    and violence, 44

K

Kapvay®, 145
Kayla, transcript of telephone conversation with, 155–161
Kindling theory, 114–115
Kraepelin, Emil, 27

L

Labetalol, 141

M

Manic depression, 27–28

Manic episodes, and bipolar disorder, 30

Medication

and aggressive behavior, ii

alpha-blockers, 142–144. *See also* Alpha-blockers

beta-blockers, 139–142. *See* Beta-blockers

individual adjustment of therapeutic dose, 138–139

monitoring pulse and blood pressure, 138

Metoprobol. *See also* Toprol-XL® (metoprolol)

beta-2 receptor blocking activity, 89

for rage, 85, 87, 149

Minipress® (prazosin), 143

Misdiagnosis of bipolar disorder, viii

Mood swings

and bipolar disorder, 27, 30–31

duration, 31

predictability, 31–32

versus response to social interaction, 32

N

Nadolol, 141

Nebivolol. *See* Bystolic (nebivolol)

Non-Western cultures, treatment of adrenergic rage, 96–102

Norepinephrine, 40

and alpha receptors, 53

and blood brain barrier, 91

definition, 52

distinction from epinephrine arousal state, 81–83

excessive vasoconstriction, 91

and opposing alpha and beta nuclei in lower brain, 105–106

O

Overarousal, iv

Overmedication, i

P

Parkinson disease, 92–93

Pindolol, 141

Post-traumatic Stress Disorder, 104

Prazosin. *See* Minipress® (prazosin)

Propranolol. *See also* Inderal® (propranolol)

    adrenaline over-reactivity, 78

    anxiety, 71–72, 73

    depression, 97

    heart rate, 133–134, 135

    hyperactivity, 75–76

    rage, 70–71, 77–79, 149

Psychiatric medications

    interference with thinking and reasoning, 25

    side effects, 25

Psychosis

    alpha adrenergic reactions and rage as, 90–95

    arterial intrusion, 94–95

    from excessive dopamine, 92

in Parkinson disease, 92–93

typical, 92

Psychotic break

and bipolar disorder, 29–30

definition, 27

S

Serotonin antidepressant medications, 73–74

Side effects

of alpha-blockers, 144

of beta-blockers, 141–142

of psychiatric medications, i, 25

Startle confrontations, 95

Survey of aggressive behavior symptoms, xi–xiv

T

Tenormin® (atenolol), 140

Terazosin. *See* Hytrin® (terazosin)

Toprol-XL® (metoprolol), 140

Treatment considerations

behavioral techniques, 132

diagnosis, dysautonomia unspecified, 131

working with physicians

Two types of adrenaline arousal, 48*f*

V

Violent aggression
    and adrenaline system over-reactivity, 44–45
    behavior management considerations, 49–50
    characteristics of, 21
    definition, viii
    disruptive behaviors, 22
    and instincts, 44